READING
THE BIBLE
with
TEN
CHURCH
FATHERS

READING
THE BIBLE
with
TEN
CHURCH
FATHERS

How to Interpret, Teach, and Preach
Like the Early Christians

Gerald Bray

BakerBooks

BakerBooks
a division of Baker Publishing Group
Grand Rapids, Michigan

Published by Baker Books
a division of Baker Publishing Group
Grand Rapids, Michigan
BakerBooks.com

Printed in the United States of America

Library of Congress Cataloging-in-Publication Data
Names: Bray, Gerald Lewis, author
Title: Reading the Bible with ten church fathers : how to interpret, teach, and preach like the early Christians / Gerald Bray.
Description: Grand Rapids, Michigan : Baker Books, a division of Baker Publishing Group, [2026] | Includes bibliographical references.
Identifiers: LCCN 2025014269 | ISBN 9781540905147 paperback | ISBN 9781540905345 casebound | ISBN 9781493452859 ebook
Subjects: LCSH: Bible | Fathers of the church | Christian life
Classification: LCC BR1705 .B73 2026 | DDC 270.1—dc23/eng/20250828
LC record available at https://lccn.loc.gov/2025014269

Cover design by Darren Welch Design

Baker Publishing Group publications use paper produced from sustainable forestry practices and postconsumer waste whenever possible.

26 27 28 29 30 31 32   7 6 5 4 3 2 1

Contents

Before We Begin

Who Were the Church Fathers?

The term "church fathers" describes the men who led the church in the first few centuries after the death of the apostles. Everybody knows that Jesus entrusted the mission of preaching the gospel to his disciples, most of whom became missionaries (or apostles, as we call them) after he ascended into heaven.[1] The few exceptions to this pattern are also well-known. Judas was disqualified from being an apostle because he betrayed Jesus and hanged himself in remorse. Saul of Tarsus, better known to us as Paul, was called to become an apostle later on, but he became one of the most successful evangelists and a prolific writer. His letters make up a substantial portion of the New Testament, which is the legacy of the apostles to us. Not all the New Testament writers were apostles, but the others worked in close association with them and transmitted their message. That explains why the writings of Mark, Luke, and the anonymous author of the Epistle to the Hebrews are included in the New Testament but the writers are not regarded as church fathers in the usual sense.

By AD 100, the apostles and their associates had passed away, and a new generation had taken over the leadership of the church.

They carried on the teaching of the apostles, guarding it and interpreting it to the growing number of people who were becoming Christians. For the most part, these men were pastors and evangelists who had been born into church families, though there were also some converts from paganism who mastered their new faith well enough to be able to teach it to others. They did not call themselves "fathers of the church" and were unaware that they constituted a distinct group—they were just doing their job as the Holy Spirit directed them. Many of them were later recognized as saints because they were particularly successful at what they were doing, but some of them never made it that far. Either they fell afoul of the church after their deaths and were condemned as heretics (like Origen), or they were so obscure that they were never properly identified (like Ambrosiaster).

But by the seventeenth century, the contributions of all the great teachers and writers of the early church—not just those of the so-called saints—were being recognized, so today these men are grouped together as church fathers: those who interpreted the Bible and formulated the main doctrines of Christianity as we know it today. They were not Catholic, Protestant, or Orthodox in the modern sense because they lived and worked before those divisions occurred, but all Christians today can see something of ourselves in them. We are their children—different from them in some ways, but dependent on them as our common ancestors in the faith.

When Did the Church Fathers Live?

The centuries the church fathers lived in can be divided into two quite different periods. The first period is the time when the church was persecuted by the Roman authorities and Christians were often put to death for their faith. That lasted until Christianity became a legal religion in 313, when the emperor Constantine I (306–337) granted toleration, but it was another decade or so before he controlled the whole of the Roman Empire and the church was really free. The period of persecution came to an end just before the First Council of Nicaea (325), when church leaders met to work out how they would operate in this new situation.

The second period is that of the great councils of the church, which continued and expanded the work of the First Council of Nicaea. It was not until 380 that Christianity became the only legal religion of the Roman Empire, a decision that was ratified by the First Council of Constantinople in the following year. Later on, the need to reaffirm Christian teaching and explain it in greater detail led to the summoning of further councils at Ephesus in 431 and at Chalcedon, a suburb of Constantinople, in 451. After that, the western part of the empire disintegrated under the impact of barbarian invasions, which ushered in what we now call the Middle Ages.

The eastern half of the empire did not suffer that fate and survived in diminished form until 1453, although by then it had changed greatly from what it had been in earlier times. Today we call this later empire "Byzantine" because it was ruled from Byzantium, a city that Constantine renamed after himself (Constantinople) and that is now called Istanbul. There were further councils summoned to meet there in 553 and in 680–681, as well as a later one held at Nicaea in 787, but although their decisions have been recognized by most of the Christian world, the writings of the men who composed and defended them tend to be classified by modern scholars as "early medieval" rather than as "ancient."

Whether the writers and leaders of this later time can be called church fathers is a matter of debate. Some people say that the patristic era, as it is called, lasted until about 800, while others believe that it ended earlier, perhaps about the time of the rise of Islam after the death of Muhammad in 632. For our purposes, we can say it was already coming to an end by about 500, when the western Roman Empire had broken up into the kingdoms that later formed the nuclei of the modern European states.

Whatever end date we choose, most people would agree that the years between the First Council of Nicaea in 325 and the Council of Chalcedon in 451 were the golden age of patristic theology. Using mainly Greek at first but soon branching out into Latin and then into Syriac, Armenian, and Coptic (the vernacular language of Egypt), the fathers of the church produced a vast array of material for use in training the masses of people who were streaming into their congregations.

Many of them were bishops of local churches and are now known primarily for that. For example, Gregory of Nyssa headed up the church in that small Cappadocian town; Theodore of Mopsuestia did the same in Cilicia; Augustine was bishop of Hippo, which is now Annaba in Algeria; and Theodoret was bishop of Cyrrhus, which lay in eastern Syria. None of these men came from the places they are now associated with but ended up as bishops there, and their writings reflect the ministry they had both to their own congregations and to the wider church.

Cyril of Alexandria was somewhat exceptional in that he became bishop of his native city, and John Chrysostom (whose name, meaning "golden-mouthed," was first given to him a century or so after his death) ministered in two places, Antioch and later Constantinople, where he was forced out because of his criticism of the imperial family. The anonymous Ambrosiaster probably lived in Rome, though he never held an ecclesiastical office. For a long time he was confused with Ambrose, bishop of Milan, and thus identified as a bishop, even though he was not one. Jerome was the true outlier, though—irascible in temper and eccentric in many ways, he would not have been tolerated as the leader of any church, even if he had wanted to be one! Unlike the others, he lived out his days in Bethlehem, surrounded by his books and a host of mostly female admirers, making him unique among the men now recognized as fathers of the church.

What Did the Church Fathers Do?

The first and most important thing that the church fathers did was collect and codify Christian teaching as it had been handed down to them by the apostles. The New Testament writers were inspired by the Holy Spirit, but they were not conscious of the fact that they were writing canonical Scripture. Their Bible was the Old Testament, which they had inherited from the Jews and which Jesus had used as the authority for his teaching and mission. It was only later that the Gospels and Epistles that they wrote and that we now regard as Scripture were acknowledged as having the same level of authority in the church as the Hebrew Bible had. This did not happen because anybody decreed it but because the books that form our New Testament virtually imposed themselves on Christian congregations that heard God speaking in and through them. At first, not all of them were accepted as canonical by everybody, either because their authorship was uncertain (such as Hebrews or Revelation) or because they did not circulate everywhere in the Roman world (such as 2 and 3 John and Jude). But any doubts were soon overcome, and by the fourth century, most churches were using the New Testament as we know it today. A canon of Holy Scripture—the Word of God—had come into being, and it has stood the test of time.

The church fathers facilitated this development by preaching sermons on the recognized canonical books and writing commentaries on them. Their sermons and commentaries circulated among the churches and established the New Testament texts as authoritative for teaching Christian beliefs. The same process was at work with the Old Testament, as the Hebrew Bible was known in the church. But most Christians had no knowledge of Hebrew, so they had to use Greek translations instead. These Greek versions often contained extra books that were not part of the Hebrew Bible, and their status as Holy Scripture was uncertain. Today we call these books the Apocrypha, and they are sometimes printed in our Bibles as supplements to the Old Testament, but were they ever recognized as writings inspired by God? The Jews never accepted them as such, and the early Christians were unsure what to do with them.

That was the subject of a debate between Jerome, the great translator of the Bible into Latin, and Augustine of Hippo, the most prolific theologian of ancient times. Augustine argued that because the New Testament usually quotes the Old Testament from the Greek versions, they should be accepted as the church's standard, Apocrypha and all. Jerome replied that the Old Testament had been revealed to the Jews and therefore it was up to them to decide what its contents should be. The medieval church sided with Augustine, but the Reformers of the sixteenth century revived the opinion of Jerome (along with the study of Hebrew), which is why Protestant churches have adopted the Hebrew canon and not the Greek one.

This sometimes makes a difference, as in the numbering of the Psalms, for example. The Greek versions use a slightly different system, with the result that most of the Psalms have a different number—what we call Psalm 119, for example, is Psalm 118 in the Greek canon. Sometimes the books have different names from the ones we are used to; 1 and 2 Samuel, for example, are 1 and 2 Kingdoms, followed by 3 and 4, which to us are 1 and 2 Kings. The church fathers used the Greek system, and modern editors of their texts are inconsistent—sometimes they follow the fathers without comment and sometimes they adjust the names and the numbering to make them fit with what we are used to now.[2]

In trying to decide what to do with the Old Testament, the church fathers used the Greek texts, with the corresponding numbering system and names, but wrote commentaries only on the books recognized by the Jews as part of the Hebrew Bible, and not on the Apocrypha. This tells us that those extra books were not being used in the preaching and teaching ministry of the church. Even if they were present in the manuscripts that the churches had, they did not function as Scripture the way the Hebrew Old Testament did. The church fathers may not have realized it, but in practice they established the Hebrew canon as authoritative in a way that the Apocrypha was not. Today that distinction is generally recognized even by the Roman Catholic and Eastern Orthodox churches, which accept the Apocrypha as part of their Old Testament. They call those books "deuterocanonical," or of secondary status, not rejecting them completely (as Protestants usually do) but not giving them unjustifiable authority either. We can thank the church fathers for that solution to the question, even though they were not conscious of what they were doing at the time.

The church fathers also worked out what the basic teaching of the Bible was and how it should be presented to the church at large. Their legacy is known to us today mainly through the creeds, or symbols of the faith, which stand as monuments to their labors. The most well-known of them is the Apostles' Creed, so called not because it was written by the apostles but because it reflects apostolic teaching as the church fathers understood it. They gave priority to the doctrine of God, which is why the creed is structured in a trinitarian way—a clause about God the Father, a section about God the Son, and a word about God the Holy Spirit. This creed probably grew out of statements that new believers were asked to affirm at their baptism—you could not become a church member unless you signed on to them!

The second major creed is usually called the Nicene Creed because it was thought to have originated at the First Council of Nicaea in 325. We now know that to be incorrect. It first appears in the surviving records at the Council of Chalcedon in 451, and the best guess is that it was composed at or shortly after the First Council of Constantinople in 381. For that reason, it is sometimes called the Nicene-Constantinopolitan Creed, which is quite a mouthful, so the shorter term "Nicene Creed" has tended to prevail in popular usage. It is more detailed than the Apostles'

Creed, but because it was ratified by church councils, it is also more authoritative as a statement of Christian doctrine. It was composed by church fathers and defended by them against all challengers, making it the most widely accepted confession of faith in the Christian world today. If you want to know what orthodoxy is (as opposed to heresy), this is the place to start—and we have the church fathers to thank for it.

There is also a third creed, commonly known as the Athanasian Creed. It was named after but not actually composed by Athanasius, who was bishop of Alexandria from 328 to 373 and a staunch defender of orthodoxy. As far as we can tell, it was written in Latin (which Athanasius probably did not speak) sometime in the late fifth century, a hundred years or more after his death. It is much longer and more systematic than either of the other creeds, and, in many respects, it is not really a creed at all. Its structure is different, and it was probably intended for teaching more advanced students the basics of the Christian faith. It has a place in some Protestant churches but is not commonly used in public worship. Roman Catholics also affirm it but do not make much use of it either. The Eastern Orthodox churches do not recognize it at all. Even so, it represents what the fathers of the Western (Latin-speaking) churches believed around the year 500, and, in that sense, it is a useful summary of patristic doctrine as it was taught and received at the close of the golden age of early church theological thought.

Why Do the Church Fathers Matter?

The church fathers were not directly inspired by God, as the writers of the New Testament were, and so they do not enjoy the same authority. They occasionally contradict each other (and even themselves!), they are sometimes mistaken in what they say, and there are a lot of questions that they never addressed in the way we would expect a modern theologian to do. It is hard to appeal to them to decide matters like the role of women in ministry, the place of charismatic gifts in worship, or the role of the church in our modern, pluralistic society. Some of them may have touched on matters like these, but if they did, it was not their main concern, and to quote them in support of some modern position is to take them out of context. This is true, for example, if we appeal to them when trying to interpret biblical passages like the creation narrative in Genesis 1–2, which most of them approached in ways that seem strange to us and are inapplicable to modern debates about evolution.[3] These limitations have to be recognized and accepted for what they are—we cannot expect men who had no electricity to come and rewire our house!

But to dismiss the church fathers as obsolete and therefore irrelevant to our modern concerns is going too far. We accept the authority of the Scriptures, which are even older and equally ancient in terms of modern society and culture, and the church fathers were much closer to the world of the prophets and apostles than we are. They may not have understood them completely, but chances are they had a better perspective than we have today because they shared much the same mentality and assumptions.

The fathers are also responsible for the broad outline of Christian doctrine that we teach and preach today. They were the ones who worked out what it means to say that Jesus Christ is fully God and fully human. They were the ones who came up with the right way to express the relationship between the Father, the Son, and the Holy Spirit as a Trinity of divine persons who nevertheless are only one God. Every major Christian church is committed to these formulations of biblical teaching, whether they recognize that or not, and those who do not agree, like Jehovah's Witnesses, for example, are not regarded as Christian denominations by anyone except themselves. The line between orthodoxy and heresy is drawn according to the way the church fathers defined it, and that principle is applied in practice by everyone from the Eastern Orthodox churches at one end of the spectrum to the Plymouth Brethren or the Churches of Christ at the other end.

The fathers are also the ones who set the boundaries between the church and Judaism on the one hand and between Christianity and paganism on the other. As Christians, we revere the revelation given to the Jews in the Old Testament and see ourselves as having been grafted into the tree that is Israel, but we are not Jews. Even less are we pagans, however much we may admire the achievements of the ancient Greeks and Romans. We acknowledge our debt to them in almost every field of human knowledge and experience, but not in religion, where they have nothing to offer us. In fact, when we read a pagan writer like Plato, for example, it is often with a sense that the great philosopher rejected the polytheism that surrounded him and often preferred to speak of "God" in the singular, even though he did not know anything about Israelite monotheism. But if we do this, we are following the example of the church fathers, who frequently saw their pagan ancestors as people who did the best they could without divine revelation, but whose conclusions had to be rejected when the light of truth dawned in the gospel of Christ. The fathers were evangelists to a pagan world they set out to conquer, and in this respect we follow in their footsteps. For that, if for no other reason, we remain in their debt.

How Should We Approach the Church Fathers Today?

This book is an introduction to the church fathers, not a definitive or encyclopedic study of them. If they were all included, it would be several volumes long, and there would be disputes about who should (and who should not) be studied in detail. Some who would have to be mentioned are almost unknown to us, and it is hard to know what to say about them. Others have dubious reputations and were accused of schism or heresy either during their lifetime or later. Probably most of them would attract little interest outside specialist circles. The average reader could easily be lost in a maze of "facts" that are often hard to pin down or be blown away by details whose importance for the wider church is not immediately obvious. A selection has to be made, and we must admit that choosing only ten of the more prominent fathers will not be uncontroversial. Many will think that some undoubtedly important people, like Athanasius of Alexandria, ought to be included, and will wonder why they have been left out. Others will think that men like Irenaeus, Tertullian, and Cyprian of Carthage deserve a place at the table and will be unhappy that they too have been passed over. How can our very limited choice be justified?

For this short introduction, the main criterion of selection has been the contribution that particular fathers have made to the interpretation of the Bible. It is true, of course, that all of them were engaged with the Scriptures because those were the foundational documents of the church. Without the teaching and preaching of the biblical message, there would have been no Christianity at all! But for different reasons, some fathers have left us a greater legacy of commentary and interpretation than others have. Occasionally this is accidental. Origen, for example, wrote an enormous amount on different parts of Scripture, but much of it has been lost. Sometimes there are other explanations. Irenaeus, Tertullian, and Athanasius all tackled the great heresies of their time and made extensive use of the Scriptures in refuting them, but they were not expositors of the sacred texts the way John Chrysostom or Theodoret of Cyrrhus were. They made use of the Bible when it suited their purposes, but they cannot be regarded as interpreters of it in the way that systematic commentators or preachers were.

We have chosen this criterion of contribution to biblical interpretation not just because preaching and teaching the Scriptures was of central importance to the early church, but also because it is still of central importance to the church today. It is here, more than anywhere else, that we stand alongside the church fathers. We do not share their culture, we do not speak their languages, and we often do not appreciate their priorities. But we do share their principles, we speak (and listen!) to the same God they did, and we agree with them that our preaching and teaching should be determined and directed by the Word of God.

Ultimately this is why the church fathers matter to us and why we have to be ready to hear their voices. We may disagree with them on many things, just as we disagree among ourselves, but they are our brothers in the faith that we share, and we believe that they have gone before us to a place where we all shall spend eternity. We should therefore get acquainted with at least some of them as we wait to join them around the throne of glory in praise of the one God who is the Lord and Savior of us all.

In the pages that follow, we will look at ten important interpreters of Scripture whose writings shaped the understanding of the early church. Two of them lived in the time of persecution and suffered because of it. Seven of them wrote in Greek, the main language of patristic theology, and the other three in Latin, which became the language of the Western church in the Middle Ages and continues to influence us today. Two of them were honored in their lifetimes but condemned as heretics centuries after their deaths. Very few took the trouble to learn some Hebrew, though almost all of them were deeply learned in the Old Testament and tried their best to interpret it as a collection of prophecies that were fulfilled in Jesus Christ.

They took different approaches, some of which modern readers find more congenial than others, but all of which have contributed to the ongoing life of the church. One way or another, they represent the entire scope of patristic thought, from the most appealing to the most bizarre. But however we look at them, they were men of God who were doing their best to understand his plan of salvation in Christ and to interpret it for a world in need of his gospel. That need has not changed and in some respects is greater than ever. We can learn from the church fathers what our own mission must be and take heart from their experience that even if we sometimes fail to get it right, God will honor and bless his faithful servants as they strive to live for him.

Timeline

Latin West	Greek East

AD 100 Justin Martyr born

AD 165 Justin Martyr died

AD 185 Origen born

AD 254 Origen died

CHRISTIANITY LEGALIZED
AD 313

First Council of Nicaea
AD 325

AD 335 Gregory of Nyssa born

Jerome born *AD 347*

AD 349 John Chrysostom born

AD 350 Theodore of Mopsuestia born

Augustine born **AD 354**

Ambrosiaster flourished *AD 366–384*

AD 376 Cyril of Alexandria born

CHRISTIANITY BECOMES SOLE OFFICIAL RELIGION
AD 380

First Council of Constantinople
AD 381

(continued)

AD 393 Theodoret of Cyrrhus born

AD 395 Gregory of Nyssa died

AD 407 John Chrysostom died

Jerome died **AD 419**

AD 428 Theodore of Mopsuestia died

Augustine died **AD 430**

First Council of Ephesus
AD 431

AD 444 Cyril of Alexandria died

Council of Chalcedon
AD 451

AD 458/466 Theodoret of Cyrrhus died

Second Council of Constantinople
AD 553

Third Council of Constantinople
AD 680–681

Dates in italic are approximate.

1

JUSTIN MARTYR

(ca. AD 100–ca. 165)

Who He Was

Justin was born into a pagan Greek family in Nablus (near Samaria) around 100. He grew up in a place that would have been familiar to Jesus and must have known something of the New Testament world, though things had changed in the century that separated the two men. Then, too, the Greek colonists in Palestine had little to do with the native population whose language they did not speak and whose customs they did not appreciate. More importantly, Jerusalem had fallen to the Romans in 70, and the temple had been destroyed, two events that put the New Testament world beyond the reach of Justin's generation, although when he was young there were still plenty of Jews in Palestine. They were to revolt again in 132, when Justin was already a grown man, and he would have known all about the final destruction of their community, even if he was not directly involved in it. He must have met Samaritans all the time, but there is no sign that he had much to do with them. He knew a few words of Aramaic, the language they spoke, but that was all.

His education and background were entirely Greek, and in his younger days he looked for consolation and intellectual satisfaction not in the religion of his native land but in different Greek philosophies, each of which reflected the beliefs of a particular philosopher or philosophical school—Stoicism, Aristotelianism, Pythagoreanism, and, above all, Platonism, to which he felt a special attraction because he thought it was especially similar to Christianity. None of these proved to be satisfactory, however, and eventually he stumbled across a Christian who led him to faith in Jesus. But even after his conversion, he did not display any particular interest in retracing the steps of Jesus and his disciples, although he could easily have done so. The Jewish world of Palestine remained a closed book to him despite his interest in evangelizing Jews—cross-cultural communication was not something he practiced or even understood!

Once he became a Christian, Justin matured rapidly in his new faith and soon became a teacher to others. At some point he moved to Rome, where he started a school, but he was betrayed by his enemies and put to death there, perhaps around 165. His reputation as a martyr was such that he was remembered for that more than anything else, but this should not obscure his considerable intellectual achievement. Justin was the most accomplished defender of Christianity of his generation, although most of his writings have been lost. What has survived are two treatises addressed to pagans and one that purports to be a dialogue between him and a Jewish rabbi, whom he calls Trypho. Trypho may perhaps be identified as Tarphon, a well-known rabbi of the time, but whether Justin ever met or debated with him personally is hard to say. Just as his treatises addressed to pagans were probably read (and were certainly preserved) only by Christians, so his dialogue with Trypho may have been a set piece designed to reinforce a Christian understanding of the Old Testament rather than to convince a Jew to accept it.

Be that as it may, Justin's writings give us a valuable insight into the way that the church conducted its evangelism a hundred years after the death and resurrection of Christ. It was two-pronged. On the one hand, Justin had to address the dominant culture of the time, which was the classical pagan civilization of Greece and Rome. Few pagans would have known anything about Judaism or the Bible, even though it was available in Greek, so the thrust of his evangelistic approach was directed toward paganism itself.

Justin—and here he was in the company of many other Christians of his time—was adept at pointing out paganism's inconsistencies and inability to make sense of the world and its problems. In sharp contrast to that, Christianity offered a coherent vision of a universe created and controlled by a single God, who had responded to the rebellion of his human creatures by sending his Son to die for them. That had been predicted by the Hebrew prophets of old, but just as importantly for Justin and his readers, it had also been foreshadowed by the great pagan philosophers of the past who had perceived elements of the truth without being able to make sense of them. Today we might say they were like people trying to do a jigsaw puzzle without the picture to guide them, and so we should not be surprised if they put many of the pieces in the wrong place by mistake.

Justin and the Jews

Justin criticized the incoherence of paganism, an approach that gained him considerable sympathy among the philosophically inclined, who often thought the same thing, but he did not stop there. He claimed not only that Moses and the Hebrew Bible were more ancient than the writings of the Greek philosophers, which was largely true, but that the latter had got their best ideas from the Jewish prophets, which would have been technically possible but is highly improbable. Where the philosophers differed from the prophets, Justin claimed that the Greeks had misunderstood them: "Everything the philosophers said about the immortality of the soul, punishments after death, the contemplation of heavenly things or similar teachings, they were able to understand and explain because they took their cue from the prophets. This is why there appear to be seeds of truth among them all, but whenever they contradict themselves they are shown to have misunderstood them."[1]

The philosophers' mistakes were not their fault, however, because until the coming of Jesus, the meaning of the prophecies was unintelligible even to Jews.[2] Given that many Jews refused to believe that the Old Testament had been fulfilled in Christ although they had regular access to the prophecies that foretold him, it is hardly surprising that pagan intellectuals would also reject him in spite of the evidence that was plain for them to see.[3] Justin did not hesitate to quote many of those prophecies, some of which were particularly obvious. He placed great emphasis on the virginal conception of Jesus, foretold in Isaiah 7:14 and also mentioned in Micah 5:1–2, which claimed that the Messiah would be born in Bethlehem, the original home of the great king David.[4] Here, of course, he was doing no more than repeating what the New Testament already said.[5]

Whether Justin knew the apostles or not is uncertain, but he did refer to what he called the "memoirs" of the apostles, which were called Gospels, and would appear to have been the Synoptics (Matthew, Mark, and Luke).[6] Justin also quoted a long series of sayings of Jesus, all of which are found either in Matthew or in Luke (or occasionally in both). Some scholars have thought that this indicates that Justin had access to a collection of Jesus's sayings that was also used by the Evangelists, but this is uncertain.[7] It is true that he did not quote anything else from the Gospels, apart from the fulfillment of Old Testament prophecies, but that does not prove that he did not know them. He had to select his material, and for an audience that was used to hearing the proverbs and aphorisms of great pagan thinkers, producing something similar from the lips of Jesus may have seemed the best way for him to persuade pagans to listen to him.

More remarkable, at least from a modern point of view, is the fact that Justin did not explicitly cite the letters of Paul or the other apostles, though many of his references to the prophecies are paralleled in them and Justin may have drawn on their example.[8] What is certain is that he never quoted noncanonical texts or introduced sayings of Jesus that are not recorded in the Gospels. That does not prove that he knew them, but it does at least indicate that he did not stray from what was, or would soon be, officially recognized as genuine apostolic teaching.

Justin was different from other intellectual evangelists of his time—or "apologists," as they are called, because they wrote justifications ("apologies") for Christianity—in that he reached out to Jews in a way that they didn't. For that reason, he paid special attention to the interpretation of the Old Testament, which he believed was sufficient to prove that Jesus Christ was the Messiah, or Savior, promised to the Jewish people. The result is that we have a kind of commentary on the Hebrew Bible, the first one to be written after the Epistle to the Hebrews in the New Testament and a precious indication of how a second-century Christian read the Jewish Scriptures and applied them to Christ. Justin could not use the New Testament for that purpose, partly because it did not yet exist in its present form, but mostly because his Jewish dialogue partners would not have recognized its authority. Here Justin was following in a tradition that he had inherited from earlier generations, one that went back to Jesus himself. Just as Jesus opened up the Old Testament Scriptures to the men on the road to Emmaus, so Justin did the same a century later and with the same intention—to prove that its promises had been fulfilled in the life, death, and resurrection of Christ.[9]

Justin used the standard Greek version of the Hebrew Bible, the Septuagint, as his main text, which was still acceptable to most contemporary Jews, although they were increasingly dissatisfied with it and were producing other translations that were closer to the original.[10] Study of Justin's quotations has shown that he was aware of those efforts and was able to use at least one of these "corrections" himself, which shows that his knowledge of Judaism was not as superficial as we might think. This may be where his Palestinian origins helped him, and perhaps it indicates that he had real contact with the Jewish communities he grew up around, but we cannot be sure of that. What we do know is that Justin presented his dialogue with Trypho as a friendly encounter in which each one respected the other. The dialogue does not end with Trypho's conversion but with the hope that they might continue their discussion later, as both Jews and Christians sought to understand the true meaning of the scriptural prophecies. That in itself reveals a friendly attitude toward Jews and Judaism that would not become common again until modern times, and it gives Justin a relevance to interfaith dialogue that we would do well to study as we seek to share the good news of Christ with the ancient people of God.

How Justin Read the Bible

In examining Justin's use of the Old Testament, it is essential to understand that he saw it primarily as a book that points to Christ, whether literally or in some less obvious sense. Justin did not draw hard-and-fast distinctions between the plain meaning of the text and the various kinds of figurative language that it might contain. For him, the literal and the figurative merged into one another almost imperceptibly. Sometimes the message was clear, as in Isaiah 7:14, which speaks of a virgin who will conceive and bear a son. Since there was no other example of a virginal conception, Justin was convinced that this verse could only refer to the birth of Jesus.[11] Similarly, Justin did not hesitate to quote Isaiah 53 as a straightforward account of Christ's crucifixion since, once again, there did not appear to be anyone else it could apply to. Justin also took Isaiah 53 as a picture of the Passover lamb, which was the Old Testament prototype of Christ, the Lamb of God who was slain at the Passover season.[12] The two things were connected, of course, because Jesus was put to death around Passover, so Justin's linking of them was only to be expected, and it made a good theological argument in the face of Jewish opposition. Not surprisingly, these two passages from Isaiah recur frequently in Justin's writings, and they were the key to the interpretation of the other prophecies, which were not nearly as straightforward.[13]

A good example of a more obscure prophecy can be found in Isaiah 8:4, where the prophet foresaw that the power of Damascus and Samaria would be destroyed in the presence of the king of Assyria. That literally happened in the lifetime of Isaiah, but Justin saw it as a prophecy that would be fulfilled by the coming of the wise men to Judaea at the time of Jesus's birth. Justin claimed that the king of Assyria was a type of Herod, because both were wicked and predatory. He also claimed that the wise men came from Arabia, because Damascus was then regarded as an Arabian city. Samaria does not fit the comparison nearly as well, but Justin overlooked that. To him, the gifts brought by the wise men were the spoils of Damascus (Arabia) and that was good enough in his eyes for them to have fulfilled the prophecy. This interpretation of Isaiah 8:4 is doubtful, to say the least, but Justin saw nothing wrong in twisting it to suit his purpose.[14] The reason for that was simple. According to Justin, all the prophecies were shrouded in mystery and could only be discerned spiritually by those who understood their messianic purpose. If they were fulfilled in Christ, as Justin believed all the prophecies were, it was inevitable that their true meaning would not be revealed until centuries after they were given. What mattered to Justin was that they were all fulfilled in the same way—by the life, death, and resurrection of Jesus Christ.

Justin was skating on thin ice at this point, but that did not stop him. He was quite prepared to indulge in pure fantasy, as when he identified the offering for lepers with the Lord's Supper,

27

or claimed that the twelve bells on the robe of the high priest stood for the twelve apostles.[15] He could even say that the scarlet cord that Rahab the prostitute displayed in her window was symbolic of the shed blood of Christ.[16] Here and elsewhere it is clear that he had been carried away by his imagination, but in his mind that was justified by the same underlying principle—the Old Testament was primarily a book of prophecies that were fulfilled in and by Jesus. How he arrived at his conclusion was much less important than the fact that he was somehow able to get there. If Trypho could be persuaded by the more straightforward prophecies that Justin was right, then presumably he would be able to swallow the rest, however fanciful some of Justin's interpretations might have seemed.

The Limits of Israel's Understanding

Another important theme that underlies Justin's reading of the Old Testament is his belief that God had accommodated his revelation to suit the limitations of Israel's understanding. This belief echoes Hebrews 1:1–3 in the New Testament, where it is stated that God had spoken to his ancient people at different times and in different ways, all of which were inferior to his full and final self-revelation in his Son. The various commandments of the Mosaic law were types and shadows of this final revelation to come. They had been given to Israel in an attempt to overcome the barriers created by human sinfulness and the inability, even of God's chosen people, to keep the law of righteousness. Circumcision, for example, had been given to them as a reminder that natural procreation was subject to the overriding power of God and a promise of future salvation, so when that salvation finally arrived, circumcision was no longer necessary, or even meaningful.

Justin also believed that Christ had existed as the Son of Man in heaven before his incarnation on earth, so he interpreted the various Old Testament theophanies as revelations of him. It was Christ who met with Abraham at the oak trees of Mamre,[17] Christ who wrestled with Jacob at the brook of Jabbok,[18] and Christ who spoke to Moses in the burning bush.[19] Once again we are dealing with Justin's imagination, though he would undoubtedly have seen his approach as similar to what the apostle Paul said about the rock that accompanied the Israelites in the desert, which was Christ (1 Cor. 10:4). Here, more than anywhere, we see the blurring of the lines between the literal and the figurative, and if Justin seems to have gone too far in many instances, it must be admitted that his interpretations were not entirely without New Testament precedent.

It is easy to find fault with the exaggerated allegories that we sometimes find in Justin, and even in ancient times there were interpreters who recoiled from the extremes they found in him. But this should not detract from the main points that he was making, as many of them are as valid today as they were when he first made them. Trypho expressed the perplexity that many Jews felt when they looked at Christians. On the surface, Christians appeared to be genuine God-fearers who worshiped Yahweh just as they did and accepted the same sacred texts as divinely inspired. But unlike Jews, Christians saw no need to separate themselves from their pagan neighbors, nor did they observe the many feasts and fasts that the Bible laid down. How then could they claim to be obeying God, when so much of what they did appeared to ignore or even go against his Word? To this Justin answered that the covenant God made with Moses at Mount Sinai had been nullified by Christ and that this had been foretold by Jeremiah, whom he quotes: "Behold, the days are coming, declares the LORD, when I will make a new covenant with the house of Israel and the house of Judah, not like the covenant that I made with their fathers on the day when I took them by the hand to bring them out of the land of Egypt."[20]

Somewhat oddly from our point of view, Justin does not go on to cite the rest of the prophecy, which spells out that in the promised new covenant people will move from performing external rites that do nothing to change a person's mentality to an inner transformation, in which the ancient law of Moses will be written on their hearts and produce a change of behavior that can only be the work of the Holy Spirit. But although he did not say that in so many words, the implication was clear. He said, "We have been led to God by Christ crucified, and we are the true spiritual Israel, the descendants of Judah, Jacob, Isaac and Abraham, who, even though he was uncircumcised, was approved and blessed by God because of his faith and was called the father of many nations."[21]

The point that Justin was making was that Jews were ignorant of the true meaning of the law, not just because Christians said they were but because their own prophets had condemned them for it. The sad result of that ignorance was not only that Jews refused to accept Christ but that they persecuted Christians for having understood what the law meant and for having received the power of the Holy Spirit to live according to its principles, even though they no longer followed the letter of the old covenant.[22]

Trypho also claimed that Christians misunderstood the messianic prophecies by associating them with the humiliation of Christ on the cross rather than with the triumphant descent of the Son of Man on the clouds of heaven. To Jews, the Messiah would be a conquering king, not a suffering servant, and it was hard for them to connect that idea with the crucified Jesus.[23] To his credit, Justin recognized there was a difficulty here, and he resolved it by saying that the prophecies would be fulfilled in two stages. In the first stage, the Messiah would come as a humble man, preaching the kingdom of God and then suffering for the sins of the world. This was the message of passages like Isaiah 53 and Psalm 22, which Justin quoted and expounded at length.[24] But the prophecies also spoke of a triumphant return in glory, and Justin placed great emphasis on that as well, quoting at length from Psalm 72 and appealing to the strange figure of Melchizedek, which the Jews did not know how to interpret.[25] The expectation of the second coming of Christ was a constant theme of Justin's apologetic, and one that he did not hesitate to use when speaking about the catastrophic state of the Jews after the revolt of Bar-Kochba, which he contrasted with the progress of Christianity among the pagans:

> Since the coming and death of our Jesus Christ in your midst, you have not had a prophet, nor do you have one now. Moreover, you no longer live under your own king, for "your land has been made waste, and abandoned as a lodge in a garden." And the Word, speaking through Jacob, "And he shall be the expectation of nations" signified figuratively his two comings, and also that the Gentiles would believe in him, which you can now certainly verify as a fact. For we Christians, made up of all nationalities, have become God-fearing and righteous through our faith in Christ, and we look forward to his second coming.[26]

Last, Trypho also pointed out that there were many false Christians in the world and wondered why that was the case. Here Justin was confronted with a real embarrassment that has plagued the church through the ages, but he did not shrink from it. Instead, he quoted the words of Jesus, who predicted that there would be many who would come in his name and spread false teachings. That was a reality even in New Testament times, and by the second century there were people who had established schools and churches in which they taught and preached their perverse doctrines. Justin acknowledges that Trypho's negative observation was a just one, but he replies, "The fact that there are such men . . . who pretend to be Christians and confess the crucified Jesus as their Lord and Christ, yet profess not his doctrines, but those of the spirits of error, only tends to make us adherents of the true and pure Christian doctrine more ardent in our faith and more firm in the hope that he announced to us."[27]

There were many wrong ways of interpreting the Christian message, but there was only one right way, and Justin believed that he had found it. The verdict of history is on his side. His name is remembered to this day, whereas those he condemned as heretics have disappeared—a warning to those who would go astray and a consolation to those who are puzzled and disconcerted by this unhappy phenomenon.

Justin's Legacy to Us

Justin's reputation has suffered through the ages, partly because he was a pioneer in the work of intellectual evangelism, and pioneers lack clear guidance. Those who came later often found fault with him, either because he was too enthusiastic in his allegorizing or because he was vague on points of doctrine that had become matters of controversy after his death. This is the inevitable fate of pioneers, and he should not be judged too harshly because of that. More seriously, he has been criticized for his negative attitude toward the Jews, which some have claimed initiated a tradition of anti-Semitism that culminated in the Holocaust of the twentieth century. It is certainly true that Justin regarded the Jews of his day as rebels against the Word of God, but, in saying that, he was doing no more than quoting the Hebrew prophets who thought the same thing.

Justin has also been accused of fomenting persecution of Jews on the grounds that they persecuted Christ and his followers, but that is a misunderstanding. Justin was living at a time when Christians were being persecuted by the Roman authorities, and he knew what suffering was. When Trypho objected that Jews also suffered persecution under the Romans, Justin could point out—correctly—that that was because they had rebelled against the empire. Also, they perhaps were not cognizant of their relative privileges: Jews had been free to worship in a way that Christians never were, but in spite of that, they were in decline while the church was flourishing. It is certainly the case that after Christianity was legalized the church took advantage of its status to discriminate against the Jews, but Justin can hardly be blamed for things that happened two hundred years and more after his death.

A better perspective on Justin's approach to Jews can be found in the *Dialogue with Trypho* itself. As he and Trypho parted, neither man having been able to persuade the other, they concluded their encounter: "After this they left me, wishing me a safe voyage and deliverance from every disaster. And I in turn prayed for them, saying, 'I can wish you no greater blessing than this, gentlemen, that, realizing that wisdom is given to every man through this way [of life], you also may one day come to believe entirely as we do that Jesus is the Christ of God.'"[28]

This is the true spirit of Christian evangelism, and a lesson that speaks to us with as much force as it did to those who first heard it. Justin made his mistakes, as we all do, but on the things that really matter he struck the right note, and we can still learn from him how to think about our Old Testament inheritance and apply it in the teaching and preaching of the church today.

● REFLECTION QUESTIONS ●

1. Are Christians right to find prophecies of Christ in the Old Testament?
2. Is Christianity something more than pagan philosophy or Judaism, or is it completely different? Can we use one or both of them to argue for the truth of the gospel?

● FURTHER READING ●

Translated Texts of Justin Martyr

Barnard, Leslie W., trans. *The First and Second Apologies.* By Justin Martyr. Paulist Press, 1997.

Falls, Thomas B., trans. *Dialogue with Trypho.* By Justin Martyr. Catholic University of America Press, 2003.

Studies

Aune, D. E. "Justin Martyr's Use of the Old Testament." *Bulletin of the Evangelical Theological Society* 9 (1966): 179–97.

Barnard, Leslie W. *Justin Martyr: His Life and Thought.* Cambridge University Press, 1967.

Cosgrove, Charles H. "Justin Martyr and the Emerging Christian Canon: Observations on the Purpose and Destination of the Dialogue with Trypho." *Vigiliae Christianae* 36 (1982): 209–32.

Osborn, Eric F. *Justin Martyr.* Mohr Siebeck, 1967.

Skarsaune, Oscar. *The Proof from Prophecy: A Study in Justin Martyr's Proof-Text Tradition: Text-Type, Provenance, Theological Profile.* Brill, 1987.

2

ORIGEN

(ca. AD 185–ca. 254)

Who He Was

Origen was a Greek speaker born into a Christian family at Alexandria sometime around 185. He was able to take advantage of the best education that the ancient world could offer and was well-schooled in the philosophical currents of his time, especially in the variety of Platonism that was then emerging. He was tutored by a pagan philosopher called Ammonius Saccas, who later taught Plotinus (ca. 204–270), the man who is usually credited with being the first representative of what we now call Neoplatonism, a reinterpretation of Plato's original teaching that gave it a certain mystical and semireligious tinge. Whether Origen and Plotinus ever met is unknown and probably unlikely, though they both represent the intellectual milieu of their time, albeit in different ways. Plotinus developed Platonism along lines that are remarkably similar to Christianity, but he never embraced the faith for himself. By contrast, Origen dedicated his life to systematizing

Christian beliefs to a degree that had not been attempted before. He was cooler toward Platonism than most of his contemporaries, but he was nevertheless marked by his philosophical training, which would cause problems for his legacy in the centuries following his death.

Origen began his career in inauspicious circumstances. His father Leonidas had taught him the basics of Christianity but was martyred in 202. Left without resources because his father's property had been confiscated by the state, he was forced to support himself by teaching. As it happened, the bishop of Alexandria took the eighteen-year-old under his wing and made him head of the catechetical school that he had managed to revive after the persecution. Origen was a very popular and successful teacher, not only because of his ability to communicate his subject matter to his students but also because his way of life reflected the seriousness with which he took the message of the gospel. He went from success to success, winning over many pagans and heretics in the process and establishing his school as the leading source of Christian teaching at the time.

During his years in Alexandria, Origen traveled to different parts of the Roman Empire, visiting the capital around 212 and later visiting Antioch and parts of Arabia. These latter journeys are of particular interest because it appears that Origen was invited to Antioch by the emperor's mother and to Roman Arabia by its governor, both of whom wanted to hear what he had to say. If these reports are correct, they show that persecution had given way in establishment circles to curiosity about the new faith. Unfortunately, trouble came to Alexandria a few years later when the emperor Caracalla closed all its schools, and around 216 Origen left for Palestine. There he was invited to lecture, but his bishop Demetrius of Alexandria objected, apparently on the grounds that Origen was a layman. The Palestinian bishops rectified this by ordaining Origen, but that merely infuriated Demetrius, who excommunicated him and revoked his ordination. Origen sought to return to Alexandria after Demetrius's death in 232, but the new bishop upheld the excommunication, and so he went back to Palestine, where he founded a new school at Caesarea Maritima.

It was at Caesarea that Origen spent the most fruitful years of his career, which were cut short by renewed persecution in 251. Origen was arrested and tortured but was not put to death. When the persecution ended, he was released from prison, but his health never recovered, and he died shortly afterward. During his lifetime he made friends and enemies in roughly equal numbers, but after he passed away, his authority as a teacher and theologian was uncontested even by those who disagreed with him. Whether they wanted to or not, every subsequent Christian writer would owe an enormous debt to Origen, who shaped the pattern of Christian theology for centuries afterward.

His influence was not without controversy, however, which flared up periodically. Around the year 300 he was accused of bowing to Platonist theories about the origin of the human soul, though the matter was confined to academic debate and did not affect his reputation in the wider church. A century later, it was a different story when Jerome, the great Latin translator of the Bible, turned against Origen's allegorizing tendencies after having initially been impressed by his works. Jerome's about-face caused a rift between him and his associate Rufinus, who was responsible for a number of translations of Origen's writings into Latin, but once again the controversy did not have a lasting impact. However, misgivings were also being expressed by leaders of the Greek-speaking churches, like Epiphanius of Salamis and Theophilus, the bishop of Alexandria, who both condemned aspects of his teaching. Finally, in 553, the Second Council of Constantinople issued fifteen anathemas against him, which determined the fate of his reputation.

Whether Origen was guilty of the charges laid against him is a difficult question to answer. The centuries after his death were a time of intense theological debate about the Trinity and the incarnation of Christ, and questions that had not been thought of in Origen's time became matters of controversy. Inevitably, Origen would be found wanting, and by taking some of his remarks out of context, a case could be made against him. But Origen himself was always determined to remain within the boundaries of the church's official teaching, and he cannot be blamed for interpretations of his writings that were formulated centuries after his death and in quite different circumstances. Today, most scholars agree that although Origen did say some things that were open to misunderstanding or that could be read in conflicting ways, he was not a heretic in the true sense of the word. We can read what he wrote, bearing in mind the difficulties that some of his statements were later to cause, but at the same time accepting that in his own context he was doing his best to affirm the truth of Christianity.

Origen's Writings

Unfortunately, the condemnation of Origen in 553 led to the widespread disappearance of most of his writings, particularly in the Greek-speaking world. Some were actively destroyed, while others were simply neglected, but either way they vanished from sight. By contrast, the Latin translations made by Rufinus and others have mostly survived, allowing us to access what Origen had to say to a degree that would be impossible otherwise. By any standard of measurement, Origen was the most prolific ancient Christian author by far. We know the titles of about eight hundred of his works, but the true figure was much higher, reaching at least two thousand and perhaps as many as six thousand treatises in all, though this last number seems to be an exaggeration. Whatever the case may be, what we now have is only a fraction of his total output, but it is enough to give us an idea of his greatness. It is also enough to make it plain that interpretation of the Bible lay at the center of Origen's teaching, even though few of his sermons or commentaries have survived.

Of his nonexegetical writings, the most important is his extensive refutation of the Platonist philosopher Celsus, which survived in its entirety. This is somewhat ironic, since Celsus's own treatise, known as the *True Discourse*, has disappeared. Celsus wrote it around 178, before Origen was born, but it seems that it went largely unnoticed at the time. It wasn't until about 246, nearly two generations later, that one of Origen's students brought it to his attention and asked him to compose a refutation so that Celsus's arguments would not damage the spread of the Christian faith. Origen was reluctant to agree to that, believing that it would be better simply to let Celsus fade into obscurity, but he was eventually persuaded to change his mind. The result was that his response to his pagan opponent contains so many quotations from him that it is possible to reconstruct most of what Celsus wrote! Nevertheless, *Against Celsus* is a seminal work, the greatest defense of Christian faith in the ancient world and an effective rebuttal of its pagan critics. Modern readers may find some of Origen's arguments unconvincing, but there can be no doubting his overall achievement, remarkable for its time and still of some value today.

Other writings by Origen include a treatise on prayer, one on martyrdom, and another on the meaning of Easter, all important themes in early Christian writing. There is also the transcript of a debate with an Arabian bishop by the name of Heraclides, which took place around 245. Heraclides had difficulty understanding the Trinity, and Origen did his best to clarify the issues involved, though he lacked the sophisticated terminology of a later time. What he said was that the Father and the Son were two gods who had a single power. He knew that such a formula was bound to scandalize a convinced monotheist like Heraclides, and he took great pains to explain how it was possible for the Father and the Son to be distinct while at the same time being only one God. We can tell from the way he approached this question that he was looking for a way to say that Father and Son were two persons in one nature but did not have the vocabulary he needed to express that properly. The *Dialogue with Heraclides*, which was rediscovered as recently as 1941, is a good example of how orthodox Christian doctrine is often latent in the church's teaching before it is properly defined. Origen knew what he wanted to say but lacked the words he needed to say it, words that would only come after years of discussion and debate.

Another of Origen's nonexegetical works is his *First Principles*, an introduction to Christian theology—the earliest of its kind and a model for much that was to come later. The original Greek is mostly lost, but it survives in a Latin translation that Rufinus edited by modifying some of its potentially controversial passages. Even so, what we have is a faithful representation of Origen's overall approach and an important introduction to the methods of his biblical interpretation. It is interesting to note that the book consists of four parts, dealing in turn with God, the world, human freedom, and divine revelation. This fourfold division of subject matter was to survive into later times, being copied in the twelfth century by Peter Lombard in his *Sentences* and in the sixteenth century by John Calvin in his *Institutes*. The content may have changed to some extent, but the form it was presented in has had a remarkable durability that is still noticeable today.

How Origen Read the Bible

Origen was the first person who can properly be called a textual critic of the Bible. With an exemplary systematic approach, he reproduced the entire Old Testament in six parallel columns, which is where the name of the work, the *Hexapla*, came from. The first of these was the Hebrew text; the second was the same text in Greek letters; the third was a Greek translation done by a man called Aquila sometime in the early second century AD; the fourth was another Greek translation produced by Symmachus early in the third century AD; the fifth was the Septuagint translation made at Alexandria from the third to the first century BC; and the last was the version of Theodotion, dating from about AD 180.

Origen not only knew all of these, but his selection shows that he was up-to-date with the latest research, since the translation of Symmachus was done in his own lifetime. How far Origen read or understood Hebrew is a matter of debate, but at least he realized its importance and took great pains to point out where the Septuagint (in particular) differed from it. He was also aware of possible mistakes made by translators when transcribing Hebrew names, which shows that he was sensitive to the nuances of the Hebrew, whether he fully understood the language or not.[1] A work of the size of the *Hexapla* was not easily reproduced, but the manuscript was housed in the library at Caesarea, where it remained for hundreds of years. Jerome consulted it when preparing his Latin translation in the late fourth century, and short extracts from it have been preserved in other writings. The original seems to have disappeared at the time of the Muslim conquest of Palestine in the 630s, but that it managed to survive that long is remarkable.

The *Hexapla* is a monument to Origen's preoccupation with textual accuracy. Given that he was later accused of playing fast and loose with the Old Testament, it is important to understand this aspect of his work. Origen believed that the text contained metaphorical meanings, but he also believed that in order to grasp them accurately it was necessary to have the best possible literal readings. In this respect, the Bible might be compared to a riddle where it is important to get the right clues if the puzzle is ever to be solved. Origen did not use that analogy, but it gives us an idea of how he looked at the question and why it mattered so much to him.

Origen was a great preacher, but of the 574 sermons that he is known to have preached, only about half have survived in whole or in part, and most of those are in Latin translations. No more than twenty-one are extant in Greek, of which twenty are on Jeremiah, along with fragments of several others. As for the

Latin sermons, we have several on the Pentateuch (except Deuteronomy), Joshua, Judges, Psalms, Song of Songs, Isaiah, Jeremiah,
and Ezekiel. There are also thirty-nine on Luke's Gospel, which
were translated by Jerome, plus portions of his sermons on Job,
1–2 Samuel, 1–2 Kings, 1 Corinthians, and Hebrews. As far as
we can tell, it appears that Origen's sermons, geared as they were
to poorly instructed members of the church, concentrated more
on the basic teaching of the Christian message and less on the
kind of moral exhortation that more advanced believers might
be expected to absorb, but this is a relative emphasis and not a
strict separation of interest. Origen had to meet his congregations
where they were and lead them on to higher things, much as a
modern pastor also has to do.

Origen was also the first Christian to write biblical commentaries, though none of them have survived in their original form. Of
his commentary on Matthew, only eight of the original twenty-five
books survive in Greek, with a Latin translation filling in much
of the rest. Similarly, we have only eight of the original thirty-
two books of his commentary on Luke. We are more fortunate
with Romans, in that Rufinus translated and abridged the fifteen
original books into ten, but they cover the entire epistle. Rufinus
also left us four of the original ten books of commentary on the
Song of Songs.

Everything else has been lost, apart from a few fragments
preserved in different places. From catalogs that others made
in ancient times, we know that there were once commentaries
on Genesis, 1–2 Kings, Isaiah, Lamentations, Ezekiel, the twelve
Minor Prophets, Galatians, Ephesians, Philippians, 1–2 Thessalonians, Titus, Philemon, and Hebrews, but they have all disappeared. The loss is irreparable, although because many later Greek
writers borrowed heavily from Origen, his impact can still be felt
in the commentary tradition of the church fathers.

What can we say about Origen's biblical interpretation based
on the little that has come down to us? Fortunately, we do not

have to rely only on the sermons and commentaries, important as they are, because he explained his methods in his *First Principles,* especially in the fourth book. From that we can glean that Origen followed the approach already adopted by Justin Martyr and others of an earlier generation. This means he read the Scriptures on two levels, the literal and the figurative, or spiritual. But while his predecessors had done that more or less instinctively and on an ad hoc basis, Origen was systematic. He not only read the texts the way his predecessors did, but he gave reasons for doing so and elaborated principles by which he believed the correct level of interpretation could be decided in any given case. In that respect, his work was an advance on what had gone before and would become foundational for what lay ahead.

When approaching the Scriptures, Origen began with the belief that they are the permanent incarnation of Christ. For him, the treasure hidden in the field (Matt. 13:44) is Christ or the Bible—the two things were effectively the same to him.[2] The link between them was obvious: Both Christ and the Bible are described as the Word (Logos) of God and therefore they can be identified with each other. Moreover, the words of the Bible are themselves the words of Christ, given to the prophets (Old Testament) and apostles (New Testament) and containing the sum of Christian teaching.[3] Even as a purely historical document, the Old Testament contains clear prophecies of the coming of the Messiah, which even the Jews accept as genuine, and which Origen claimed were fulfilled in Jesus.[4] Origen explained the fact that not everybody could see this by saying that just as the Messiah was covered in Mary's flesh, so he was hidden in the Bible under the veil of the literal sense of the text.[5]

It was the duty of the exegete to remove that veil and demonstrate, by an appeal to the higher senses of Scripture, what treasures it was concealing. This could only be done by the inspiration of the Holy Spirit, the true author of the sacred texts, who gave the gift of illumination to his chosen teachers who were few in number, but of whom Origen was clearly one.[6] Why this gift of illumination should be restricted to a chosen few, Origen explained by saying that the treasure the Scriptures contained was too valuable to be scattered indifferently to every passerby. His argument was taken from the words of Jesus in the Sermon on the Mount, when he said that it was wrong and dangerous to cast pearls before swine.[7]

Finding Christ in the Old Testament

There was no contradiction in Origen's mind between Christ and the Holy Spirit, both of whom were considered authors of the Bible, because of their inner-trinitarian relationship. To put it succinctly, the Spirit reveals the hidden things of God, and those hidden things are Christ, so the authorship of the Scriptures can be attributed to both of them working together.[8] The common work of Christ and the Holy Spirit was also the foundation of the unity of the two Testaments, which Origen had to defend, not only against the Jews, who rejected the New, but also against the Gnostics and Marcionites of his own time, who either rejected the Old or relegated it to an inferior status. In effect, Origen was fighting on two fronts. On the one hand, he had to demonstrate that the Old Testament was not the fullness of the revelation given in Christ and that to rely on it alone, as the Jews did, would be to miss its true meaning. On the other hand, to ignore or downgrade the Old Testament would be to uproot the gospel from its moorings in the creation and in the law of God, making it effectively meaningless.

Origen achieved this balancing act by drawing comparisons between the Testaments that illustrated how the New complemented and fulfilled the Old. For example, he described the Old as a time of sowing seed and the New as the time of harvest.[9] Similarly, whereas the Old Testament was the light of a lamp, the New Testament was the light of the sun.[10] He frequently referred

44

to Moses as the schoolmaster leading us to Christ, a theme that can trace its origins to the apostle Paul.[11] There are many other examples of this approach, but the point is that Origen insisted that the two Testaments were in basic agreement with each other, and therefore of equal value as revelations from God.[12] If the Old Testament was more obscure in some places than the New was, it was the duty and the calling of interpreters inspired by the Holy Spirit to make its meaning plain.[13]

To do this successfully, Origen had to start with the assumption that because the Bible was the word of Christ, every part of it was useful and made sense in its context.[14] Furthermore, its message was centered on Christ, which meant that, in the case of the Old Testament in particular, it was often necessary to look beyond the literal text to the spiritual meaning it concealed. The discoveries that resulted from this deeper reading had to be meaningful both to the interpreter and to their listeners, who were expected to hear the Word of God and obey it. But we must not be misled into thinking that Origen undervalued the literal sense of the text or thought some kind of allegorical interpretation had to be imposed on it if it were to make sense to Christians. As he himself says, "We must say . . . that in some cases we are well aware that the historical facts are true. For example . . . Jerusalem is the capital of Judaea, where a temple was built by Solomon, and thousands of other things like that. The passages that are historically true are far more numerous than those that were written with purely spiritual meanings in view."[15]

It was important for Origen to emphasize this point because those who were converted to Christianity almost always began with the literal reading of the Scriptures and wanted to know whether what they said had actually happened in history. Christians couldn't accept that the life, death, and resurrection of Jesus, for example, were literary inventions, even if some aspects of the Gospels (like the parables) fell into that category. That there was a real God who was active in human affairs set Christianity apart from pagan mythology and was basic to the proclamation of the gospel message of salvation. The spiritual senses of Scripture might be added to that, and in some places the literal meaning of the text could not be accepted as it stood, but they were the exceptions, not the rule, which is important to keep in mind. As long as Christ was present in the literal sense of the text, Origen saw no need for allegory—the literal and the spiritual were one and the same. It was only when the message of Christ was less obvious on the surface that he appealed to a more allegorical kind of interpretation, though always with an eye firmly fixed on what was made clear elsewhere in the Bible.

From the Letter to the Spirit

In seeking to realize the task of spiritual interpretation, Origen was guided by the Platonic belief that reality had two dimensions, the material (literal) and the mentally intelligible (spiritual), which to him was the same as what Paul said about the difference between the letter of the law and its spirit.[16] He firmly believed that he was following in the footsteps of his apostolic predecessors, and if pagan sources happened to coincide with them, as Platonist ones sometimes did, then that was because God had graciously allowed some pagans to get a glimpse of his glory without revealing the fullness of the truth to them. That was the approach already adopted by Justin Martyr and others, and Origen was happy to follow it.

To the basic distinction between the literal and spiritual senses of Scripture, Origen added an additional component that would become characteristic of much later biblical interpretation. This was the moral sense, which in principle was accessible both to Jews and pagans and did not require the degree of spiritual perfection that was available only to Christians.[17] Origen compared these three levels of interpretation to three parts of the human being— the literal sense to the physical body, the moral sense to the soul,

46

and the spiritual sense to the human spirit.[18] Whether Origen was successful in making a real distinction between the moral and the spiritual senses has been doubted by many modern scholars, some of whom have denied the existence of the moral sense altogether, while others have claimed that because what Origen thought of as the moral sense was understandable to both Jews and pagans, it was not really Christian at all. But a careful examination of the evidence shows that these objections are unfounded.[19] Origen was very clear in his mind that a real difference existed between the moral and spiritual senses of the text and that the former was just as Christian as the latter, even if it was shared to some extent by those outside the faith.

To illustrate his theory, Origen cited the example of the apostle Paul, who used the Old Testament prohibition against the muzzling of the ox that treads out the corn to insist that a pastor should be paid for his services.[20] Origen also claimed that this was only one of several such examples that Paul used to make moral pronouncements, although he did not go into specific detail. Elsewhere he not infrequently gave both moral and spiritual interpretations to a particular passage, as when he expounded the story of Abraham being called to sacrifice his son Isaac.[21] In the spiritual sense, Isaac was regarded as a type of Christ crucified, whereas in the moral sense he was a picture of the soul that offers itself in sacrifice to God and so grows in virtue. Both interpretations focus on Christ as their center—the first objectively, in that Christ died to save us in a way that the historical Isaac never could have done, and the second because it encourages us to imitate Christ by self-sacrifice in the service of God. Here we see how all three senses come together. The literal sense is historically accurate but does not achieve its object, the spiritual sense is the fulfillment of the promise of redemption made to Abraham, and the moral sense gives the practical application of that sense to our own Christian lives.

The moral sense may appear to be squeezed in between the literal and spiritual ones, but it played an important role in Origen's pastoral practice. As he expresses it, "It is not the spirit that sins . . . it is the soul which either 'sows in the flesh' or 'in the spirit,' and which can either go to ruin in sin or be converted away from it. The body is the result of whatever the soul chooses, and the spirit is its guide to virtue if the soul wants to follow it."[22] In other words, the soul, which includes the mind, is the place where good and evil intersect in human beings, and it must decide which way it will choose. If it decides to follow the desires of the flesh, it will cut itself off from God and lead to destruction, but if it turns away from them and looks toward spiritual things, it will open itself up to the salvation that God has provided in Christ. Jews and pagans might seek this spiritual salvation, but because they are either ignorant of Christ or have rejected him, they cannot obtain it. This is why the gospel message is aimed at the soul, which holds the key to the right ordering of human life.

From Principles to Practice

It should be noted that Origen's way of applying the biblical texts in his sermons alters the logical order of the senses as he presented it in his *First Principles*. There we move from the lower to the higher in an orderly progression, but when we come to the sermons that he preached, we often discover that it is the moral sense, and not (as we might expect) the spiritual one, that comes out on top. Why is that? A clue can be found in the way he treated the story of Noah's ark. Noah was commanded by God to build an ark with three decks in it, each of the decks representing (according to Origen) one of the senses of interpretation.[23] The idea that Noah's ark is a type of the church in which people are saved from destruction was not new to Origen, of course—something like it can be found in the New Testament, and it quickly became a stock image in Christian teaching.[24] But Origen developed it by saying that the lower deck was the place where the animals were kept, the animals being types of the ordinary members of the church, both in their variety and in their relative incomprehension of the mysteries of the faith. The upper deck represented the soul, exposed to the elements of nature and challenged to confront them with all the skill it could command. The middle deck was the place of safety, where Christ the captain of our salvation dwells, and the place where the spiritually alert want to gain access.

Christ is in the middle for two reasons. The first is that he is the center, the core whose essence is protected by the lower and upper decks that surround it. The second is that he holds the other two together. Those struggling on the upper deck might not appreciate it, but the less advanced believers in the lower deck are also part of the church and will be saved with it in the end. It is the duty of the more enlightened ones to encourage them to glimpse the glory of Christ and be encouraged to engage in the spiritual warfare that preoccupies those on the upper deck. That some come to this awareness more slowly than others should not surprise us, because people move at different paces. As Origen puts it, "Every soul receives and absorbs the Word of God according to its own capacity and faith. But once souls have absorbed the Word of God and implanted him in their minds and understanding . . . then they are attracted to him as to the odor of a divine perfume. Being filled with new strength and speed, they run after him as fast as they can, and hasten to enjoy the odor of his sweetness."[25] In other words, the slow learners may look unpromising, but they should not be written off!

Here we see the great difference between Christians on the one hand and Jews and pagans on the other. Jews and pagans were putting their trust in a two-layer ark, a lower one for beginners and a higher one for those trying to lead a moral life, either by keeping the law of Moses or by following some philosophy or other. But neither of them was aware of the third level hidden between the other two, and therefore they had no assurance of salvation. Christians, on the other hand, were those who had seen the glory of Christ and who were motivated by that to engage in a spiritual struggle that had eternal life with him as its goal. Christians were not trying to save themselves by their morality but were driven to seek moral rectitude by the vision of the Savior that they had received.

Here there is an uncanny resemblance to what the sixteenth-century Reformers called "the third use of the law." The law of Moses had been given first, to show what God requires of his people, and second, to condemn them for not being able to keep it. But those who had been saved by putting their faith in Christ could go back to the law and, in the power of the Holy Spirit, strive to keep it as best they could in imitation of Christ himself. As Origen says, "We who read or hear these things should pay attention to both parts—to be pure in body, upright in mind, pure in heart, reformed in behavior. We should strive to progress in our deeds, to be vigilant in knowledge, faith and action, and to be perfect both in our deeds and in our minds, so that we may be worthy to be conformed to the likeness of Christ's sacrifice, through our Lord Jesus Christ himself."[26]

That there is not a clear separation between the two levels of spiritual understanding corresponds to the difficulty of distinguishing the soul from the human spirit, but the basic distinction was that the level of the soul spoke to the Christian life in this world, whereas the level of the spirit spoke of the eternal joy and rest that is the heavenly reward of the faithful believer. The spiritual sense also pointed to the future hope of Christians that had not yet been fulfilled but would be realized in the second coming of Christ.[27] Wise man that he was, Origen did not have much to say about the book of Revelation, which remained a mystery to be revealed at some future time, but he acknowledged that and found a place for it in his overall scheme of interpretation.

From these basic principles, Origen went on to explain their various nuances. For example, in the case of the Song of Songs, the bridegroom is Christ the Logos, but the identity of the bride is less clear. At some times she appears to be the church as a whole, but at others she seems to be a representation of the soul of the individual believer. This duality is not a contradiction, however, because the church is made up of individuals and what applies to each one applies equally to the community. Origen knew that and said as much at the beginning of his commentary on the book.[28] The same is true of Israel's crossing the Red Sea in Exodus 14:1–31. This event symbolizes both baptism, which is the common experience of all Christians, and the death of sin, which has to be realized in the soul of every individual believer. Once again, there is no contradiction here—the one implies the other.[29]

Historical Truth and Spiritual Meaning

In addition to such dual applications of the moral and spiritual senses, there are passages of Scripture that Origen regarded as being defective at the literal level. That is to say that the text says things that are either impossible or highly improbable. Origen actually made a list of the more important of these, beginning with the creation of the sun and moon on the fourth day—impossible, because days are measured by the sun and the moon—and continuing to the command of Jesus that if a man's right eye causes him to sin, he should tear it out and throw it away.[30] Rather than attempt to find a literal interpretation for such passages, Origen had recourse to the spiritual level as the right one on which such statements should be read. He even went to the point of claiming that God had put such verses into his Word so they would stimulate the curiosity of readers and encourage them to go deeper in order to come up with the true meaning, drawing closer to him in the process.[31]

The need for multiple levels of interpretation is more prevalent in the Old Testament than in the New, but Origen saw that they came together in the life and ministry of Jesus. Without denying the historical truth of the events described in the Gospels, Origen insisted that many of them had a spiritual significance that could not be ignored. For example, the healing miracles of Jesus were manifestations in the body of what was even more necessary in the souls of those who came to him.[32] The resurrection of Lazarus symbolized the resurrection of the soul from the death of sin, a point that is not mentioned in John's Gospel but can plausibly be inferred from the words of Jesus pertaining to the promise of eternal life to all believers.[33] Origen claimed that even the transfiguration demonstrated the diverse ways Jesus makes himself known to people according to the capacity and needs of each individual.[34]

Origen believed that the Gospels were susceptible to this kind of spiritualization that could in principle be applied to everything in them, a conviction that seems to go beyond anything that the Gospels themselves encourage.[35] Was this a logical inference, or good intentions gone mad? Both interpretations are possible and demonstrate the kind of ambiguity that would later call his methods into question. But of his intentions there can be no doubt. Jesus told the Pharisees, "You search the Scriptures because you think that in them you have eternal life; and it is they that bear witness about me" (John 5:39). Origen believed he was doing no more than taking what Jesus said at face value and applying it to everything that the Bible records about him.

Summarizing the achievement of a man like Origen is difficult to do in a short space, but perhaps what strikes us most is his ability to operate with equal dexterity in the academic world and in the congregations of the church. In his *First Principles*, we see a clearly developed scheme of biblical interpretation set out with examples taken from both Testaments and joined together in a logical sequence. In his sermons, on the other hand, we see how he was able to adapt his principles to the needs of his hearers and minister to them pastorally. We may find it hard to accept some of his ideas, and the loss of so much of his work makes it difficult to know just how representative what we still have actually is, but even when we allow for a certain margin of error, there can be no doubting his genius or his desire to be faithful to his calling. Those who studied under him or heard him preach would doubtless have been struck by his genius, but they would not have been led astray, because however different he may have been from us, his heart was in the right place, and we can rest assured that the cause of Christ, so dear to him, was greatly advanced as a result.

The Pastor Theologian

Origen's life and work were so varied and complex that it is impossible to summarize their importance in a few sentences. Even though most of what he wrote has been lost, what remains is still more than most people can easily digest. Was he a saint or a heretic? Did he point the way to the future, or did his speculations and allegorical methods lead subsequent generations astray? These questions have been asked for centuries and answered in different ways, often unfavorably. But whatever conclusions we may come to, in the end there can be no escape from his influence, because in one way or another, all roads lead back to Origen.

He was the first Christian to write commentaries on the Bible, a tradition that continues to the present time. What is more, he thought of the Scriptures as a collection of texts that preach the same message because they come from the same God. To interpret one part of them in a way that devalues or rejects another part is to fall into misunderstanding, a principle that Christians still uphold today.

Origen saw clearly that the message of the Bible was to preach the gospel of salvation in Christ. Whether this was done by preparing people to receive it (Old Testament), or whether it was a proclamation of the great event after it had occurred (New Testament), the underlying theme is the same. Here, again, Christians of every age stand in solidarity with him.

He also believed it was essential to establish what the correct text of the Scriptures was and to provide adequate translations. He did not believe that the Septuagint, the Greek translation made by Jews in Alexandria before the coming of Christ, was infallible, even though he recognized its value and accepted that it had been the text most used by the apostles in the New Testament. He knew that better versions could be produced and kept up-to-date in this field, something we continue to do today.

Throughout his life, Origen systematized his study of the Bible and his exposition of the Christian faith. He preached sermons, he wrote commentaries, and he composed an introduction to his methods that was designed to make sense of the whole. Centuries later, John Calvin would do something very similar, writing commentaries on the Bible, producing (and constantly revising) an introduction to his theological methods (his famous *Institutes*), and applying his teaching in his weekly sermons. It would be misleading to call Calvin a Reformed version of Origen, but the pattern of his ministry is remarkably similar, and his impact on the church is comparable. Both men have been admired and reviled in equal measure, and in both cases, it is the aberrations of their followers more than their own errors that have led to that unhappy situation. To understand Origen is therefore to understand ourselves and the tradition in which we live as much as the one he did so much to create.

Finally, Origen insisted that Christians must grow in their faith. It is not enough to recite Bible verses. We must ask what they really mean and how we should apply them in our lives today. Everything in the Scriptures has its importance, even if that is not immediately obvious to us. Nobody is ever so completely immersed in them that they have nothing more to learn; spiritual perfection remains an ideal, but one that is beyond our grasp in this life. As Origen understood, the best is yet to come, and we will not be fully satisfied until the great day of Christ's return. In all these things and more, Origen blazed a trail that we continue to follow.

● REFLECTION QUESTIONS ●

1. How far can we spiritualize biblical texts that seem hard to interpret otherwise? Did Origen strike the right balance between what the Bible says and what it means?
2. Can a non-Christian philosophy (like Platonism, for example) help us read the Bible?

● FURTHER READING ●

Translated Texts of Origen

Barkley, Gary W., trans. *Homilies on Leviticus 1–16.* By Origen. Catholic University of America Press, 1990.

Behr, John, trans. *On First Principles.* By Origen. Oxford University Press, 2017.

Bruce, Barbara J., trans. *Homilies on Joshua.* By Origen. Catholic University of America Press, 2002.

Chadwick, Henry, trans. *Contra Celsum.* By Origen. Cambridge University Press, 1953.

Dively Lauro, Elizabeth A., trans. *Homilies on Judges.* By Origen. Catholic University of America Press, 2010.

Heine, Ronald E., trans. *Commentary on the Gospel According to John.* 2 vols. By Origen. Catholic University of America Press, 1989–1993.

Heine, Ronald E., trans. *Homilies on Genesis and Exodus.* By Origen. Catholic University of America Press, 1982.

Lienhard, Joseph T., trans. *Fragments on Luke.* By Origen. Catholic University of America Press, 1996.

Scheck, Thomas P., trans. *Commentary on the Epistle to the Romans.* 2 vols. By Origen. Catholic University of America Press, 2001–2002.

Scheck, Thomas P., trans. *Homilies 1–14 on Ezekiel.* By Origen. Newman Press, 2010.

Scheck, Thomas P., trans. *Homilies on Numbers.* By Origen. InterVarsity Press, 2009.

Smith, John C., trans. *Homilies on Jeremiah and 1 Kings 28*. By Origen. Catholic University of America Press, 1998.

Studies

Clark, Elizabeth A. *The Origenist Controversy*. Princeton University Press, 1992.

Crouzel, Henri. *Origen*. T&T Clark, 1989.

Dively Lauro, Elizabeth A. *The Soul and Spirit of Scripture Within Origen's Exegesis*. Society of Biblical Literature, 2005.

Martens, Peter W. *Origen and Scripture: The Contours of the Exegetical Life*. Oxford University Press, 2012.

Scheck, Thomas P. *Origen and the History of Justification: The Legacy of Origen's Commentary on Romans*. University of Notre Dame Press, 2008.

Torjesen, Karen J. *Hermeneutical Procedure and Theological Method in Origen's Exegesis*. De Gruyter, 1986.

3

GREGORY OF NYSSA

(ca. AD 335–ca. 395)

Who He Was

Gregory was born sometime around 335 to a Christian family in Cappadocia, a region of Asia Minor that is now in central Turkey.[1] There were ten children in the family, but we know the names of only four—a daughter called Macrina, who was the eldest, followed by three sons, Basil, Gregory, and Peter. It seems that after the untimely death of their father, Macrina became the anchor of the household, and it is certain that the younger boys looked up to her. She made such an impression on them, in fact, that after her death Gregory wrote a treatise praising her many virtues and holding her up as a model for others—and not just women—to follow. Macrina did not conform to the female stereotypes that his contemporaries expected, and Gregory admired her for that.

Gregory's older brother, Basil (ca. 329–379), later became bishop of the Cappadocian Caesarea (modern Kayseri) and was a leading defender of orthodoxy in the theological debates of the fourth century. Gregory admired him almost as much as he admired Macrina and was fully aware of how much he owed to him. He did not start writing in a serious way until after Basil died, and he saw himself as under an obligation to continue his brother's work. Gregory's younger brother, Peter, was born after their father's death and was brought up by Macrina, who was both father and mother to him. He later became bishop of Sebaste and persuaded Gregory to complete Basil's exposition of the creation, which he had left unfinished at his death, but beyond that we know nothing about him.

Of the four children, it seems that Gregory was the only one who married, possibly because there was pressure on him to continue the family line. We know nothing about his wife, but we do know that his marriage led him to write a treatise on virginity, a paradox that many have found puzzling. There is no indication that he ever divorced or abandoned his wife, nor did he become a monk in later life, as some have alleged. What appears to have happened is that, once he was married, he realized the truth of what the apostle Paul had written to the Corinthians—that a single man could devote himself to the things of God, whereas a married one was obliged to take care of his family and was not able to dedicate himself to God's service as much as he might like to.[2] Like Paul, Gregory came to see that singleness was preferable to marriage, though it was not compulsory, and although Gregory recommended it to others, he knew that he could not enjoy it himself. In modern times, some commentators have tried to portray Gregory as a misogynist or a gay man, but they have failed to find any evidence to support these claims. Like many people before and since, Gregory appreciated the value of what he could not have, and to his credit, he made no attempt to persuade others to follow his example.

In addition to his siblings, we must take account of another Gregory (ca. 330–390), a close friend of Basil's who later became bishop of the small Cappadocian town of Nazianzus. Basil and the two Gregorys were linked together in a common theological enterprise that they are still remembered for today. Basil was the leader of these Cappadocian fathers, as we now call them, slightly older than the others and gifted with an administrative ability that ensured his rapid rise in the church hierarchy. He was the first person to write a treatise dedicated to proving the divinity of the Holy Spirit, and he is also known for a detailed commentary on the six days of creation (the *Hexaemeron*), which he interpreted literally. Gregory of Nazianzus was a gifted orator and poet whose reputation in later times was such that the Greek church bestowed on him the accolade of theologian ("divine"), by which he is still known in the Eastern Orthodox world.[3] His prominence ensured that he was chosen as the president of the First Council of Constantinople in 381, but he had no aptitude for church politics, and the role did not suit him. He soon resigned and went back to Nazianzus, where he died nearly ten years later. He is remembered today mainly for his theological orations, in which he set out the doctrine of the Trinity in terms that would become standard in the Christian world.

Gregory of Nyssa was considerably younger than the other two. He looked up to Basil as his inspiration and was associated with Gregory of Nazianzus at the First Council of Constantinople, where he played a leading role. He lived longer and wrote more than they did, but his career cannot be understood apart from them. Not only did he complete Basil's unfinished *Hexaemeron*, but he also wrote an extended rebuttal of the antitrinitarian theology of someone called Eunomius, a task that Basil had started but that had been interrupted by his untimely death.

Basil and Gregory of Nazianzus studied in the philosophical schools of Athens, where they were tutored in Neoplatonism—this philosophy had developed since the time of Plotinus. Neither they nor Gregory of Nyssa subscribed to Neoplatonism in later life, but they were all influenced by it and thought in categories that derived from it. That has been enough for some scholars to claim that their theology was distorted by a pagan philosophy, but that is a misunderstanding. The Cappadocians spoke the language of Neoplatonism because it was the common intellectual parlance of their time, but the substance of their thought was very different, and in many respects they provided an antidote to it. Their Christianity was not intellectual speculation about what exists above and beyond the material universe but a revelation of the one God who had sent his Son into our world, not only to explain that heavenly reality but also to provide a means for us to enter it. To them, Neoplatonism was a theoretical idea invented by men, but Christianity was a practical experience revealed by God, and that made all the difference.

What drove the Cappadocians to write and preach the way they did was not Neoplatonism but a heresy that had emerged from within the church itself. Christianity was made a legal religion in 313 when the emperor Constantine issued an edict of toleration that was meant to apply to the entire Roman Empire. But at that time, Constantine controlled only the western provinces, and it was not until 324 that he was able to bring the eastern ones under his control. By then, a controversy had erupted in Alexandria over the views expressed by a presbyter called Arius (256–336). What Arius actually taught is unclear, because it was overlaid and obscured by positions taken by many people who were labeled "Arians" but who often differed from one another.

Arianism came in many forms, but in general terms, its adherents believed that the Son of God was divine but inferior to the Father, who was God in the absolute sense. According to the Arians, there had been a time before the Son came into existence. Some of them thought that the Father had given birth to him in order to use him to create the world. Others said that he had been latent in the Father's being as his Word or Mind (Logos). They interpreted the Greek version of Proverbs 8:22 ("The LORD created me as the beginning of his works") to mean that the Son was the first creature to have been born (NET). Like everyone else, the Arians also believed that there was an absolute difference between the Creator and his creatures and that the gap between them was unbridgeable. Only the Father was uncreated, and so only he was God in the full sense of the word. The Son shared certain aspects of the Father's divinity and so could be called "divine," but he was still a creature. Yet the expression "divine creature" made no sense. Either the Son was God, or he was not. If he was not, he could still be a messenger from God, like a kind of superangel, but not God himself. If that was so, said the anti-Arians, in what sense could Jesus Christ be called a revelation of God? How could a mere creature, however exalted or divine, be the Savior of the world?

Arianism contained a logical contradiction that eventually doomed it as a viable explanation of the incarnation of the Son as Jesus Christ. But what alternative was there? One that was popular was attributed to an otherwise unknown theologian called Sabellius, who supposedly taught what is often called "modalism." This said that the terms "Father," "Son," and "Holy Spirit" were just names given to the one God, according to the way (or "mode") in which he acted in the world. As Creator, God was the Father. As Redeemer, God was the Son. As Sanctifier, God was the Holy Spirit. They were not different beings, but one being acting in different ways. Unfortunately, this simple solution did not do justice to the evidence of the New Testament. For example, when Jesus was speaking or praying to his Father, was he talking to himself? When he said to the Father, "Not my will, but yours, be done" (Luke 22:42), who was he speaking to? Verses like that made it clear that Father and Son were not just different names for the same divine being, but how could they be told apart? Was it possible for the Son to be fully God without being the Father? And who (or what) was the Holy Spirit? Was he a second Son? Or was the word "spirit" being used simply to describe the Father according to his divine nature? The Scriptures, for example, were divinely inspired (2 Tim. 3:16), but that inspiration was the work of the Holy Spirit (2 Pet. 1:21). How should that be understood?

The answers to questions like these were not long in coming. As soon as Emperor Constantine was in control of the entire Roman world, he summoned a council of bishops to decide what to do about Arianism. This became the First Council of Nicaea, which met in 325 and decreed that the Son of God was of the same "being" as the Father. The Greek language is rich in vocabulary that can be used to express this concept of "being," but the one the council chose comes straight from the Bible itself. In the Scriptures, God is often described as the great I AM, and so the council took the word *ousia* ("being"), derived from the verb "to be," and used it to say that the Son is *homoousios* ("of one being") with the Father.[4]

But it soon transpired that *homoousios* could be interpreted in different ways. Did it mean that the Son was identical to the Father, making any distinction between them impossible, or could it be understood as saying that the Son was *like* the Father without being exactly the same as him? Think in terms of humanity. Tom, Dick, and Harry may be triplets—the same at the level of species or "being," but nevertheless identifiably different men. This is possible because there is no single generic human being who contains every characteristic of human nature. The Greek term for that was *homoiousios*, the extra *i* being the proverbial iota that made all the difference. Human beings are *homoousioi* with each other because we share a common "being," but this must be interpreted as being *homoiousioi*, because we are similar to each other without being identical. Some Arians went even further than this. For example, Eunomius—whom both Basil and Gregory wrote against—denied that the Son was like the Father at all and claimed instead that the Son was clearly inferior to him in every respect and closer to a created angel than anything else.

What about God? Are Father, Son, and Holy Spirit triplets like Tom, Dick, and Harry? Here the answer must be no, because there is only one God. You cannot be like him without actually being him. The biblical witness, however, is that while there is only one God, the Father is God, and the Son is one with him.[5] Yet "Father" and "Son" are more than just two different names for the same being. There is also the question of the identity of the Holy Spirit, recognized as a third party in Matthew 28:19 and treated as such in professions of faith that Christians had to make at their baptism, but not clearly defined in relation to the Father and the Son. Was he a coequal member of the Godhead or merely a divine force belonging to one or both of the others but inferior to them? This question touches directly on Christian experience. If we have the Holy Spirit dwelling in our hearts by faith, do we have the presence of God in our lives or just a substitute for him, a kind of ambassador from heaven who might be more exalted than the angels but not essentially different from them?

The Cappadocian fathers spent their careers trying to work all this out in what we now call the doctrine of the Trinity. Their great contribution was to establish that there are two ways of looking at God, both of which are equally valid and necessary. As a being (*ousia*), God is one and beyond human understanding. We can say that he is nothing like us, but we do not know what he is. This "negative" approach—God is invisible, immortal, and so on—is often called by its Greek name "apophatic" and is typical of the Cappadocian approach. Whatever we say about the Father at this level is equally true of the Son and of the Holy Spirit, because they share his divine being. But it is misleading to characterize Cappadocian theology as purely (or even as mainly) apophatic, or as later theologians would describe it, as mystical. There is also a "positive" or "cataphatic" dimension in that we know God in three ways—as Father, Son, and Holy Spirit. The Cappadocians called these three *hypostases* (singular: *hypostasis*), taking up the word found in Hebrews 1:3 to describe the Father in relation to the Son.

The problem was that it was difficult to define exactly how the three *hypostases* related to the one divine *ousia*. In the past, *hypostasis* and *ousia* had sometimes been used interchangeably, but that option was not open to the Cappadocians, because they could hardly say that Father, Son, and Holy Spirit were three "beings" or "substances" in the one "being" of God. The *hypostases* were not distinct from each other by their nature, which was the same for all of them, but in some other way. This, the Cappadocians realized, was revealed in their relationship to each other. They knew from Scripture that the Son was "begotten" of the Father and that the Holy Spirit "proceeds" from him, but how "generation" ("begottenness") and "procession" differed from each other, they could not say—that was a mystery hidden in God.[6] Nevertheless, it was these relations that defined the identity (*hypostasis*) of the three. The Father was "unbegotten," meaning that his identity was not determined by any other *hypostasis*. The Son was "begotten" of the Father, a term taken from John 1:14, and the Holy Spirit "proceedeth" from the Father, as Jesus told his disciples in John 15:26 (KJV).

Expressed in this way, the terms used suggested that there was some kind of action in which the Son and the Holy Spirit emerged from the Father, which sounds suspiciously Arian, but that was avoided by pointing out that the relations between the *hypostases* were eternal. There was never a time when the Son and the Holy Spirit had not existed, just as there was never a time when the Father had not yet become the Father. As far as their divinity was concerned, the Father remained the reference point for the other *hypostases*. They were divine because of their relationship to him, and he was described as the source of their divinity. How the Son and the Holy Spirit were related to each other was left undefined. They were not twins, but neither did they exist independently of each other. This unwillingness or inability to explain their relationship would later cause a rift between the Greek (Eastern) and Latin (Western) churches, because the latter wanted to insist that the Holy Spirit proceeds from the Father *and the Son*, something that the Easterners were unable to affirm. That controversy, known by the Latin word *Filioque* ("and [from] the Son") endures to the present day and is one of the main questions that still divides the two great branches of Christendom.

The creed adopted at or shortly after the First Council of Constantinople in 381, which we mistakenly call the Nicene Creed, enshrines Cappadocian theology to a large extent, and for that reason the Cappadocians have long enjoyed the reputation of being primary authorities for trinitarian orthodoxy. Eastern Orthodox theologians seldom go beyond this, but as the *Filioque* dispute demonstrates, the West has developed its theology a little further. Nevertheless, both sides honor the Cappadocians for their magnificent contribution to the development of Christian doctrine, and their inheritance is a shared treasure of the entire Christian world.

Having said that, it is also true to say that the Cappadocian fathers have been relatively neglected, something that is particularly acute in the case of Gregory of Nyssa. His works were not properly edited until the twentieth century, and relatively few translations have been made. Furthermore, those who have discovered him in modern times have frequently come to his writings with their own agenda. At their hands, Gregory has been turned into a protofeminist, a postmodern existentialist, a crypto-socialist, and any number of other things, sometimes including their exact opposites![7] This has led to an unfortunate situation in which much of what has been written about Gregory in recent years is unreliable, distorting the unsatisfactory picture we have of him still further. A truly balanced assessment of Gregory has yet to be produced, but the complexity of his work and the variety of interpretations to which it has been subjected makes it unlikely that a definitive study of him will appear anytime soon.

How Gregory Read the Bible

Gregory of Nyssa was basically a follower of Origen, as were most Greek-speaking Christian writers of his time. He did not follow the master intensively, but neither did he take part in the debates about many of Origen's theological views that were surfacing toward the end of the fourth century. Gregory felt free to use Origen for his own purposes and to go beyond (or against) him when he thought that was necessary, but he never felt pressured into taking sides for or against him. For example, in discussing the raising of Samuel from the dead by the witch of Endor, Gregory insisted that the phantom who appeared was a demon disguised as Samuel, and not the prophet himself, as Origen had claimed.[8] Gregory's reason for objecting to Origen's exegesis was his belief that a godly person could not be subject to satanic power, either in this life or in the next. His belief in the eternal security of the believer in heaven made him read the biblical text in the way he did, even though it must be admitted that Origen's literal interpretation appears to be the more accurate one. But the fear of falling victim to demons was real among Christians in Gregory's time, and it is his pastoral concern to allay that fear that is reflected in his reading of the text.

To call Gregory an Origenist is therefore somewhat misleading, though there can be no doubt about where much of his inspiration came from. But there are important differences between the two men that must also be taken into account. Unlike Origen, Gregory cannot really be called a biblical scholar. He did not write systematic commentaries as Origen did, nor did he engage in textual criticism. Nevertheless, his theology was grounded in the Bible, especially in key Old Testament texts, and cannot be understood otherwise. Modern readers may find fault with some of his exegesis, but it's impossible to deny his intentions, which are clear even in places where he wasn't directly engaged with biblical interpretation at all.

The Faith of Abraham

The key to understanding Gregory's reading of the Bible is his concept of faith. The archetype of the Christian is Abraham, whom the apostle Paul called the father of our faith (Gal. 3:6–9), and it is his journey from a pagan home to the promised land that models the earthly pilgrimage of the believer. One of the more influential Platonist treatises that was circulating in Gregory's time was the anonymous *Chaldaean Oracles*, so called because it was a commonplace of ancient thought that Chaldaea (Babylonia) was the original home of wisdom, from where the Magi had come to worship the baby Jesus.[9] Centuries before, Abraham had left the same region—Ur of the Chaldees, to be exact—and had set out in faith on a journey to a land of which he knew nothing.[10] To Gregory, this was a picture of a man who had abandoned the wisdom of this world (as found in the *Chaldaean Oracles*, for example) for a life lived according to the promises of God. Abraham did not know where he was going, but as Paul said, "We walk by faith, not by sight" (2 Cor. 5:7). This assertion, which seems obvious enough to modern Christians, was revolutionary in its time. Plato had had a concept of faith, but to him it was the lowest level of intellectual perception. The philosopher was expected to rise above such unquestioning trust (as he saw it) and inquire after the knowledge that would lead them to the supreme Mind (*Nous*).

For Gregory, on the other hand, the lowest form of human knowledge was sense perception, from which the seeker after truth could form intellectual concepts, which corresponded to the Platonic *nous*. Here the parallel with Origen is obvious—sense perception corresponds to the body, and the *nous* is the rational soul. But for both Origen and Gregory, there is a third and higher level, that of the spirit. The passage from the senses to the mind was possible for all intelligent beings, but to rise from that to spiritual understanding involved a crisis that could not come naturally but could only be a revelation from God. The seeker after truth could not rise to this spiritual level on their own; it had to be given to them. In the process of receiving it, they would have to discard everything that the world called knowledge and enter into what appeared to be deep darkness. But that darkness was in fact divine light, a paradox that can be expressed as dying to self and rising to newness of life. The means to this end is faith, the basis of our relationship with God.

By its very nature, faith is a relationship, not a doctrine or a philosophical principle. Because it is a relationship, it is in constant motion—it is a living thing that's always changing and growing, even as it remains basically the same. Abraham was justified before God by his faith, which is the true foundation of the Christian life and the key to our salvation.[11] The life of faith is exemplified in the Song of Songs, where the bride goes in and out of darkness and despair in search of the bridegroom, who is Christ. When he comes to her, all her doubts and fears disappear, and she is transformed by the presence of his love. For Gregory, the Song is not merely an allegory of the relationship between Christ and the believer; it is also a guide to spiritual experience that we are expected to follow if we want to come into the presence of God. Here it is noticeable that whereas Origen sees the bride as either the church or the individual soul, Gregory only mentions the church in passing. For him, the allegory is above all a picture of personal union with God.

Union with God

In Gregory's mind, faith is the exact opposite of what it is in Plato. Far from being an instinctive grasp of things that needs to be refined by knowledge to achieve real understanding, faith is the key to the realm above and beyond time and space perception that brings us into fellowship with our Creator. With this concept of faith, Gregory has turned Platonism on its head. It is true that one of the differences between classical Platonism and its Neoplatonic offspring is that Plotinus and his fellow Neoplatonists believed that there was a world above and beyond the Supreme *Nous* that in some respects corresponds to the divine darkness experienced by the bride in the Song of Songs. But for them, access to that world was only possible because the *Nous* contained within it something higher than itself. This might be called the "flower" or the "flame" of the *Nous*, and it enabled the philosopher to apprehend the Highest God and be united with him (or it).[12] As Plotinus had said, union with the One is achieved by "the element in *Nous* that is not *Nous*."[13] To put it a different way, this union is the result of human striving based on something already present in the human being, even if in most cases it is neither recognized nor developed.

For the Christian, however, experience of union with God cannot come from a human starting point, as if it were some element hidden in the human *nous* (mind). It must be revealed to our *nous* from outside itself, and God alone determines how and when that might happen. The means of communication between the divine and the human is the Word of God, incarnate in Jesus Christ and present in the Bible, which is the written form of the Word. The Bible speaks always and only of Christ, whose multifaceted glory is displayed on every page. The true student of Holy Scripture is necessarily a disciple of Christ, whom they will find in it if they search it diligently.

This is particularly clear in Gregory's treatise on virtue, more popularly known as the *Life of Moses*. True to his Origenist leanings, Gregory started off with a historical account of Moses, drawn mainly from Exodus and Numbers. At no point did he doubt the truth of the record, but that was not his main purpose in drawing attention to it. What interested him was what he saw as Moses's ascent to the knowledge of God, which could only be perceived by an allegorical reading of the text. For example, when discussing the circumstances of Moses's birth and early upbringing, Gregory says, "Since the daughter of the king, being childless and barren (I think she is rightly perceived as profane philosophy), adopted the child . . . Scripture allows that his relationship with her . . . should not be rejected until he had recognized his own immaturity. Profane education is truly barren, always in labor but never giving birth. What fruit . . . does philosophy have to show for being so long in labor?"[14]

Secular learning is to be rejected by the true seeker who's after virtue, but it's not quite as simple as that. Moses commanded the Israelites to "borrow" jewelry and other precious things from the Egyptians, but Gregory recognized that stealing was unworthy of God's people. He deals with this event by saying, "To some it seems reasonable that the Israelites should have exacted wages for their work from the Egyptians . . . but this justification does not excuse falsehood and fraud. . . . A higher sense is therefore preferable. It commands those who by their virtue share in free life to equip themselves with the wealth of pagan learning . . . philosophy, geometry, astronomy and so on . . . since these things will be useful when the divine sanctuary of mystery has to be beautified with the riches of reason."[15] So pagan learning is not all bad, but its riches must be put to good use in building the kingdom of God. This may not have anything to do with the historical exodus, but it is not an unreasonable thing to say in itself. Gregory knew what point he wanted to make and then found a biblical text he could make fit his predetermined requirements!

The Salvation of the Human Race

Finding Christ in the Scriptures was Gregory's aim, but as we might guess, that was not as straightforward as it might seem. Moses in the desert had a meeting with God in the burning bush. Gregory knew what he wanted to say about that: "From this we learn the mystery of the Virgin [Mary]. The light of divinity which through the birth [of Christ] shone from her into human life did not consume the burning bush, just as the flower of her virginity was not withered by giving birth."[16] Here we meet with a motif that has little or nothing to do with the biblical text, but that would dominate the thinking of the church for centuries, as

Mary was perceived to have carried God in her womb without being overwhelmed by his divinity.

We could go on in this vein for a long time. Take, for example, the creation of humanity in the image and likeness of God (Gen. 1:26–27). For Gregory, there were two creations, or perhaps two stages of one creation. In the first phase, God made a generic human, who was not sexually differentiated. In the second phase, he divided this human into male and female, making sexual differentiation a secondary matter that is not inherent in human nature. This way of thinking may sound strange to some of us, and it is hard to see that Gregory was reading the Genesis account correctly, but if we look at things from his point of view, it makes more sense than we might think. Gregory lived in a world where it was generally believed that men were superior to women, who were in some way deformed or incomplete human beings. Gregory denied that because, as Paul had said, in Christ Jesus there is neither male nor female.[17] To him that could only mean that sex was irrelevant to salvation, and since salvation was restoration to the primitive state of the human race, there could not have been any sexual differentiation in the first human creature. Although we cannot follow Gregory's exegesis of Scripture, we can agree with his conclusion—all people, regardless of gender, are equal both in creation and in salvation. In the end, we arrive at the same place he did, albeit by a different route.

It would be nice to think that this is always the case, but unfortunately it is not. Gregory is known for his belief that everything and everyone will be redeemed in the end, and he has often been criticized for it, since it contradicts the plain teaching of Scripture. But Gregory did not see it that way. To his mind, universalism, as this teaching is known, was implicit in Philippians 2:10–11: "Every knee should bow, in heaven and on earth and under the earth, and every tongue confess that Jesus Christ is Lord, to the glory of God the Father."[18] In this case, poor exegesis has not been corrected by good theology but has led instead to heresy, justified by a misunderstanding of the triumph of Christ at the final judgment.

There have been many attempts to explain this embarrassment away, but unfortunately Gregory's universalism is confirmed by what he says elsewhere: "When, after long periods of time, the evil in our nature . . . has been expelled, and when those who are now dead are restored to their primitive state, a hymn of thanksgiving will go up from all creation, both from those who have suffered punishment in the course of their cleansing and from those who needed no cleansing at all. . . . [Christ] both freed man from evil and saved even the one who introduced evil (i.e., Satan) himself."[19] Gregory did not quote the Bible to justify this statement, which is not surprising since there is nothing in Scripture to support it, but it is a reminder to us of how easily wishful thinking can come to dominate our theology and distort our reading of God's Word. There are many people today who want everyone to be saved and who interpret the Bible in a way that reflects their desire, regardless of what it actually says. Gregory is not alone!

Gregory's Legacy

Along with that of his brother Basil and their mutual friend Gregory of Nazianzus, Gregory of Nyssa's legacy persists because he explained the Cappadocian distinction between the one nature and the three *hypostases* in God. Even though their formulation of the Trinity would require further elaboration, they laid the foundation for what was to come. Without them, there is no telling how long that would have taken.

Gregory of Nyssa reminds us that Christians are justified by faith and not by their knowledge. The same theme would recur centuries later in the teaching of Martin Luther, when the alternative was not knowledge but works, but the principle is the same. Gregory insisted that the seeker after truth cannot get to God on their own but needs divine revelation. It is a constant temptation to think otherwise, and here we owe him a great debt for his faithfulness to the gospel.

He also reminds us that Christian faith is not an abstract set of doctrines comparable to a human philosophy. It is a lived experience, revealed to us in the Bible so that we may learn and reproduce it in our lives. To travel with Abraham or with Moses is to walk with God through darkness into light. The Christian life is ultimately inexpressible in mere human words; it has to be known in the heart. What was true for Gregory is just as true for us, and just as he affirmed that truth in the midst of theological controversy, so must we. We may be called to fight battles in the name of our Lord, but if so, we are called to fight them in the right way and with the right priorities, as Gregory of Nyssa did.

A final lesson from Gregory of Nyssa is that nobody is perfect— great theologians can make great mistakes. Sometimes he was rescued from his errors, as in the case of the creation of the human race, but at other times he wasn't, as his lapse into universalism demonstrates. His experience is a reminder to us of the importance of getting things right at the start. We can criticize him when we must, but we should also be prepared to learn from him so that we do not make similar mistakes. If great thinkers can go wrong, so can we, and we should learn from their errors so we don't repeat them.

● REFLECTION QUESTIONS ●

1. Is the work of a great theologian discredited when that theologian falls into error? Is it possible to distinguish the good from the mistakes, and if so, how do we do that?

2. If the entire human race fell away from God in Adam, why is it not entirely restored in Christ? What is the difference between the original creation and the new creation in Christ?

● FURTHER READING ●

Translated Texts of Gregory of Nyssa

Corrigan, Kevin, trans. *The Life of Saint Macrina*. By Gregory of Nyssa. Peregrina Publishing Company, 1997.

Malherbe, Abraham J., and Everett Ferguson, trans. *The Life of Moses*. By Gregory of Nyssa. Paulist Press, 1978.

McCambley, Casimir, trans. *Commentary on the Inscriptions of the Psalms*. By Gregory of Nyssa. Hellenic College Press, 2004.

McCambley, Casimir, trans. *Commentary on the Song of Songs*. By Gregory of Nyssa. Hellenic College Press, 1987.

Studies

Laird, Martin. *Gregory of Nyssa and the Grasp of Faith: Union, Knowledge, and Divine Presence*. Oxford University Press, 2004.

Ludlow, Morwenna. *Gregory of Nyssa: Ancient and (Post)modern*. Oxford University Press, 2007.

4

AMBROSIASTER

(fl. ca. AD 366–ca. 384)

Who He Was

Of all the church fathers studied in this book, Ambrosiaster is without doubt the most mysterious. His commentaries on the Pauline Epistles were preserved for centuries under the name of Ambrose of Milan (ca. 337–397), one of the most prominent bishops and teachers of the late fourth century, and it was not until after 1500 that the humanist scholar Erasmus demonstrated that this attribution was mistaken. When the Benedictine monks of St. Maur edited Ambrose's works from 1686 to 1690, they gave this anonymous writer the nickname Ambrosiaster, which has stuck to him ever since. More recently, another work, formerly attributed to Augustine, has been acknowledged as coming from Ambrosiaster instead, and a few further fragments have also been identified as his. But who was he?

At different times various scholars have proposed more than a dozen possible identifications, the most likely ones bearing the name Hilarius—the Roman prefect Hilarianus Hilarius, Hilarius of Pavia, or an imperial official called Claudius Callistus Hilarius, all of whom lived at about the same time. The reason for this is that Augustine quoted him as "Saint Hilary," though he was probably thinking of Hilary of Poitiers, a bishop who died in 368, and not one of these three.[1] It is quite easy to believe that Augustine confused that Hilary with another one, but which one, it is impossible to say. Internal evidence in Ambrosiaster's writings shows that he was working in Rome during the pontificate of Damasus I (366–384), which allows us to conjecture that his writings probably date from sometime in the 370s, but that is as close as we can get. He had a considerable knowledge of Judaism and took a great interest in the conversion of the Jews to Christianity, which has led some people to think that he may have been a converted Jew himself, but that is a guess with no concrete evidence, and few people are persuaded by this theory today.

Whoever Ambrosiaster was, he was well-read in Latin Christian writers, and he made frequent references to Tertullian, Novatian, Cyprian, and Marius Victorinus, all of whom lived and wrote before his time. Whether he knew Jerome is uncertain, though it is possible, and the two men may even have met during Jerome's stay in Rome from 382 to 385.[2] He did, however, mention the persecution of the church by Julian the Apostate (361–363), which he said was "recent," which confirms the general dating of his activity to the 370s or so.[3] He was also well aware that the system of church government had evolved since the time of the apostles, when presbyters and bishops had been the same thing. Remnants of that era had survived into his time in some places, notably in Egypt, but although the differentiation between bishops and presbyters was complete by his time, the memory of what had once been was still alive, which again points to the fourth century.[4]

Whether Ambrosiaster was a layperson or an ordained presbyter is unknown. His knowledge of church affairs and his frequent tendency to offer his readers pastoral advice would suggest that he was a presbyter in a local church, though he never said anything about that. Evidently he was prominent enough for his works to have been preserved, but not prominent enough for his name to have been attached to them. More than that we cannot say.

How Ambrosiaster Read the Bible

There are only two complete works of Ambrosiaster that have been identified. The first, and best known, is a running commentary on the thirteen Pauline Epistles (omitting Hebrews, presumably because Ambrosiaster did not recognize it as Pauline), which survives in two editions, with a third one for Romans. It has been thought that Ambrosiaster was himself responsible for all of them and that the third edition is the most definitive one, but of course that is speculation.

His other major work is a series of questions raised by the interpretation of both the Old and New Testaments. It also survives in three editions, containing respectively 127, 150, and 115 treatises. Most of them seek to explain difficulties encountered by readers of Scripture, but some branch into polemics against various heretics, Jews, or pagans, and occasionally into internal church politics. How these different collections were put together and by whom is unknown—it is possible, perhaps even probable, that at least some of the treatises come from other sources, but once again, we cannot say. The few additional fragments that have been identified as Ambrosiaster's touch on the Gospel of Matthew and include one on Peter's denial of Jesus. Whether Ambrosiaster wrote, or intended to write, a commentary on the first Gospel is unknown, but if the fragments are genuinely his, it is possible that he did but that it has not survived.

Ambrosiaster wrote in Latin, using a translation of the Bible that was then circulating in Italy. It was during his lifetime that Pope Damasus I persuaded Jerome to translate the Scriptures into

Latin, in what was to become the standard or "popular" version, known to us as the Vulgate. Before that came out, though, various people had made translations, which are sometimes valuable for determining what the original Greek text was. The Romans were less given to philosophical allegorizing than the Greeks, so Ambrosiaster's commentaries generally stick to the literal historical sense of the text. However, he was prepared to see Old Testament people and events as "types" of Christ and the New Testament, as long as that could be justified by rational argument. Another characteristically Roman feature of his writings is his tendency to find moral lessons in the text. The Greeks did not ignore the moral sense, but they were inclined to see it as a stepping stone from the literal to the spiritual meaning, as Origen had taught them to do. Ambrosiaster appears not to have known Origen's writings, or those of any Greek theologians for that matter, and so what we find in him is an alternative approach, more closely related to Roman law than to Greek philosophy.

Ambrosiaster was also the first person we know of who treated the Pauline Epistles as a unit and read them as the coherent thought of one man. His commentary shows that he knew the entire collection and that he read the Epistles in the same order we do. This demonstrates that the New Testament had already acquired its present shape and that it was read as canonical Scripture in the church. His concentration on Paul also shows the importance that the apostle had in the preaching and teaching of the gospel. The Epistle to the Romans in particular had become central both to the evangelization of pagans and to the longed-for conversion of the Jews. It is therefore only to be expected that Ambrosiaster should give it pride of place among Paul's epistles, but he also read it in the context of Paul's other letters, being the first Christian to have done so and to offer his readers an overview of the apostle's teaching as a whole.

Ambrosiaster began his commentary on each individual epistle with a summary of its contents as a guide to preparing his readers for what they could expect to find in it. The prefaces to Romans and 1 Corinthians are particularly full. On Romans, he said that the epistle contains four main points, which he outlined as follows:

> The first point [Paul] discusses is how [the human race] manifests itself, what it is now, what it was originally, and to whom it belongs. . . . The second point he makes is that human beings did not submit to the one God by the logic of nature, but instead engaged in dishonest and wicked activities for which they were rejected by God. . . . The third point is that they disobeyed the law which had been given to them, with the result that God preferred the Jews to the Greeks. The fourth point is that Paul teaches that when the Jews rejected Christ, they departed from the law and promise of God and became like the Gentiles, so that now both of them stand in need of the mercy of God, hoping for salvation not by the law but by faith in Christ Jesus.[5]

The prehistory of salvation is clearly outlined here, beginning with creation, followed by the fall and then the covenant with the Jews, and culminating in their disobedience. This disobedience placed them on the same footing as the rest of humanity, making salvation possible only through faith in Christ. In the preface to 1 Corinthians, Ambrosiaster listed no fewer than ten reasons why Paul wrote the epistle, all of them to do with various disorders that had arisen in the church there after his departure. The subject matter of the two epistles is thus quite different, but Ambrosiaster's approach to them was essentially the same, in that he gave his readers a checklist of what to expect as they got into the details of his verse-by-verse exposition. He followed the same pattern for the remaining eleven epistles, though his treatment of them was briefer. Even so, Ambrosiaster was the first person to preface his commentaries with such introductions, a practice that would become standard in later times.

A Rational Faith

Commenting on Romans 1:9, where Paul says that he serves God with his spirit, Ambrosiaster did not hesitate to link what Paul wrote to what Jesus said to the Samaritan woman in John 4:23–24, though with his own characteristic slant on it. He says, "Because God is a spirit, it is right that he should be served in spirit or in the mind, for whoever serves him in his mind, serves him in faith."[6] The progression of Ambrosiaster's thought is clear—to serve God in spirit is to serve him with the mind, and that is what constitutes faith. Jesus did not actually say all that, but it could be reasonably implied from the Gospel text, and Ambrosiaster did not hesitate to do so.

On the question of faith, he was very clear. Commenting on Romans 1:17, which is itself a quotation of Habakkuk 2:4, he writes, "The righteousness of God is revealed in the person who believes, whether Jew or Greek. Paul calls it the righteousness of God because God freely justifies the ungodly by faith, without the works of the law, just as he says elsewhere [in Philippians 3:9]."[7] Once again, we see that Ambrosiaster's message was clear and backed up by a reference to another one of Paul's epistles, by which means Ambrosiaster impressed on his readers the underlying unity of the apostle's thought. Ambrosiaster had no way of knowing how important this verse would be in the theological debates of the Protestant Reformation more than a thousand years later, but from what he said here, it is not hard to believe that he would have sided with Martin Luther and his fellow Reformers. What we can say is that the Reformers recognized their teaching in statements like these, which encouraged them in their belief that they were returning to the teaching of the early church.

When considering human sinfulness and God's response to it, Ambrosiaster emphasized that the punishment that God metes out to sinners isn't just what they deserve but is also a sign of his loving care for what he has made. This comes out in what he says about Romans 2:3: "God, the Creator of the world, will reward the merits of his creation with due attention and care. If God had made the world and then neglected it, he would be called a bad Creator, because he would be demonstrating by his neglect that what he had made was not good. But since it cannot be denied that God made good things . . . it is necessary to say that he is also concerned about them."[8] Later, when commenting on Romans 2:8, he added:

> Paul mentions three things which are fitting punishments for unbelief—wrath, fury and tribulation. Wrath is not in the one who judges, but in the one who is judged. . . . God is said to get angry because he is believed to take vengeance, but in reality the nature of God is immune from such passions. . . . "Fury" means that God will seek vengeance, adding to his anger the injury which has been done to him. "Tribulation" refers to the punishment which the condemned sinner will suffer. Evil is not just a matter of deeds but of unbelief as well.[9]

Here we see how Ambrosiaster was able to bring out the many-sided nature of God's wrath toward sin and sinners. The worst sins were not the misdeeds themselves but the attitudes of unbelief that lay behind them. Human beings are mandated to govern a world created by a loving God, and it is out of love for that world that God acts to punish them when that mandate is ignored or transgressed.

As for the privileges granted to Jews, Ambrosiaster says, "Paul always puts the Jew first, whether he is to be praised or blamed, because of his privileged ancestry. If a Jew believes, he will be all the more honored, because of Abraham, but if he doubts, he will be treated that much worse, because he has rejected the gift promised to his forefathers."[10] In other words, much is expected from those to whom much has been given, and the advantages given to Jews carry with them obligations that they must fulfill if they are to enjoy them properly. Moreover, as Paul points out in Romans 4:12, the privileges granted to the Jews were given to them because their ancestor Abraham believed the promises of God, and a similar gift is open to all who believe. Ambrosiaster writes, "Paul says this because by believing, Abraham became the forefather of the circumcision. But this was the circumcision of the heart, not only of those who descended from him but also of those Gentiles who believed in the way he did. He is the father of the Jews according to the flesh, but according to faith he is the father of all believers."[11]

Sin and Death

Ambrosiaster was also interested in what Paul had to say about the status of natural law, particularly during the time before the law was given to Moses. According to Romans 5:13, sin was in the world all along but was not counted when there was no law. In affirming that, Ambrosiaster says, "Before the law was given, men thought that they could sin with impunity before God, but not before other men. For the natural law, of which they were well aware, had not completely lost its force, so that they knew better than to do to others what they did not want to suffer themselves."[12]

In other words, the Golden Rule was understood and applied before there was any law at all, but it functioned only in relation to other human beings, and not in relation to God. As Ambrosiaster puts it, "It was not then known that God would judge the human race, and for that reason sin was not imputed, almost as if it did not exist in God's sight and God did not care about it. But when the law was given through Moses, it became clear that God did care about human affairs, and that in the future wrongdoers would not escape without punishment, as they had done up to then."[13]

This is an approach that seems strange to modern ears, but we can see where Ambrosiaster was coming from and why he thought in the way he did. There was indeed sin in the world before Moses, and it is fully chronicled in Genesis. Paul himself, in the very next verse, said as much and pointed out that death reigned from Adam to Moses, even over those whose sins were unlike those of Adam. Here Ambrosiaster encountered what to him was a serious logical difficulty. He could accept that death reigned from Adam to Moses, but death is still present in the world, so it cannot be said that the law abolished it. He concluded that death reigned only over those who sinned as Adam had sinned, though he swiftly added that they constituted the vast majority of the human race. This was clear to him because most people worshiped idols, which was the beginning of a death wish, as Ambrosiaster saw it.

Ambrosiaster's Limitations

As for the biblical text, which does not support this view, Ambrosiaster believed that the Greek had been corrupted at some point in the past but that the true version had been preserved in Latin. As he put it:

> Somebody who could not win his argument altered the words of the text, in order to make them say what he wanted them to say, so that not rational argument, but the authority of the text, would determine the issue. However, it is known that there were Latin-speakers who translated ancient Greek manuscripts, which preserved an uncorrupted version from earlier times . . . even the Greeks have different readings in their manuscripts. I consider the correct reading to be the one which reason, history and authority all retain. For the reading of the modern Latin manuscripts is also found in Tertullian, Victorinus and Cyprian.[14]

From this we can see that Ambrosiaster was a poor historian and that he was unable to examine the Greek originals of the texts he was expounding. Nor is this the only example of his weakness in this area. Commenting on Romans 12:11, where Paul tells the church to "serve the Lord," Ambrosiaster objected that this makes no sense. He preferred the mistranslation that he had in front of him, which said "serving time," and connected it to Paul's command for "redeeming the time," a phrase he used in Ephesians 5:16 and Colossians 4:5 (KJV). Ambrosiaster was clearly unable to let go of his Latin translation when it differed from the Greek—the thought that the original should take precedence did occur to him, but he avoided the implications of that by saying that the true original was not what the Greek manuscripts of his day said. That text had been altered, and the Latin version had preserved what Paul actually wrote, though of course he had no way of demonstrating that. It was a bad argument, but unfortunately one that would recur periodically until the Renaissance, when Greek studies were first taken seriously in the Christian Latin world.

In some other cases, Ambrosiaster read the text correctly but put a dubious interpretation on it. In the admittedly difficult case of 1 Corinthians 11:7, where Paul says that a man should not cover his head because he is the image and glory of God, whereas a woman should because she is the image of man, Ambrosiaster does some justice to the text by saying that man is greater than woman "by cause and order, not by substance," but then he goes on to say, "There is an enormous distance between the glory of God and the glory of a man, for a man is formed in the likeness of God and a woman is not. She is the likeness of God because of the man. God created only one human being, so that just as all things come from the one God, all human beings come from the one man."[15]

It is hard not to think that Ambrosiaster confused two different things here. He accepted that man and woman are not substantially different and understood that Paul was talking about their mutual relationship, not their essential origin, but by claiming that there is an "enormous distance" between them on that account is surely taking things too far. Ambrosiaster evidently could not distinguish adequately between relationship and substance, even though he recognized that they were different concepts. We understand this today, but we should not be too hard on him. That distinction was not altogether clear even to the greatest theological minds of his time, who had as much difficulty in establishing the equality of the Father and the Son, despite their difference, as they had in doing the same with men and women.

But we have to admit that Ambrosiaster did sometimes say things that reveal an underlying male chauvinism. For example, when commenting on Romans 16:13, where Paul greets a man called Rufus and then includes Rufus's mother in the greeting, he writes, "Paul mentions Rufus ahead of his mother because of the dispensation of God's grace, in which a woman has no place. For he was chosen, that is, promoted by the Lord to do his work. Nevertheless, he had such a holy mother that the apostle calls her his mother also."[16] Suffice it to say that the text does not support this interpretation!

Occasionally Ambrosiaster conflates different events, perhaps making a valid point but in a way that bypasses what the text actually says. An example of that can be found in his comment on 2 Corinthians 11:25, where Paul mentions that he had been shipwrecked three times. Ambrosiaster's take is that "the danger at sea that Paul was alluding to here was the danger that the soldiers guarding prisoners on board would kill them all rather than risk letting them swim to safety in a shipwreck. The centurion prevented this danger from materializing because he did not want Paul to be killed, but rather to be taken alive to Rome."[17] What Ambrosiaster said was true of Paul's famous journey to Rome, but it would seem to be irrelevant to the three shipwrecks that he had previously endured. This is a relatively minor slip, but one that is all the more surprising because a little reflection would have told him he was backing up his point by referring to the wrong occasion.

Living Together in Love

Ambrosiaster can be faulted on points like these, but it is important to see them in perspective. For the most part, his interpretation of Paul was full of good common sense and was basically sound. Very often, he did little more than paraphrase the apostle, perhaps adding an illustration from his own context to reinforce what the biblical text was saying. He was often at his best when enunciating general principles; for example, when he commented on Romans 13:9, where Paul talks about the commandments and sums them up by saying that what they really mean is that we must love our neighbors as ourselves, which is what Moses also said.[18] This is what Ambrosiaster had to say about that: "Moses received this writing from God in order to reform the natural law. . . . Paul means that above all the other laws there lies one which must be fulfilled in love. Although there may be other laws which Paul has not mentioned, love is the fulfillment of them all. If the human race had loved from the beginning, there would never have been any wickedness on earth."[19] A man who could write that (and mean it) can be forgiven a lot!

Nor is this an isolated remark. The theme that love triumphs over everything runs through Ambrosiaster's commentary, just as it does through Paul's epistles. On 1 Corinthians 8:11, for example, where Paul rebukes members of the church who are insensitive to their weaker colleagues, Ambrosiaster says, "The weak man will perish if he eats food which has been sacrificed to idols, because to him it goes against faith in one God. These are the words of an angry man [Paul], who is pointing out what harm can come from knowledge if it is not tempered with love. Your education is killing him . . . and so you become the cause of your brother's death when Christ allowed himself to be crucified in order to redeem him."[20]

On the question of speaking in tongues, Ambrosiaster was surprisingly evenhanded. By the fourth century, most commentators had concluded that the phenomenon had died out after the apostolic age, and they did not take it seriously. But in commenting on 1 Corinthians 14:4–5, Ambrosiaster writes, "Because he is probably the only person who understands what he is saying, the person who speaks in tongues edifies himself alone, but a person who prophesies edifies everyone, because everyone understands what he is saying. . . . Paul could not forbid speaking in tongues, because this is a gift of the Holy Spirit, but the pursuit of prophecy is more acceptable because it is more useful."[21] We cannot tell from this whether Ambrosiaster knew of congregations in which speaking in tongues was practiced, but his willingness to accept the possibility was unusual for his time and shows that he was able to interpret the biblical text without drawing unwarranted conclusions from it.

On the question of spiritual gifts in general, he was quite prepared to see them being exercised by every member of the church and not just by specially ordained officials. As he says in his remarks on 1 Corinthians 12:11, "There is only one God, whose grace is distributed to individuals as he wishes, not according to the merits of any particular person, but for the upbuilding of his church. All those things which the world wants to imitate but cannot, because it is carnal, may be seen in the church, which is the house of God, where they are granted by the gift and instruction of the Holy Spirit. They are seen in the ministries of particular individuals, so that people who are contemptible in the world's eyes may become vehicles for demonstrating the truth."[22] Ambrosiaster was a man of his time, and he had his prejudices, but on matters like these he was able to rise above his circumstances and do justice to what Paul had said, regardless of his own experience. He had a sense of objectivity that was uncommon then and still far from universal now, and that is one of the main features that give his commentaries a freshness and a relevance for today that they otherwise might not have had.

Paul's Anonymous Disciple

Ambrosiaster continues to speak to us today because he was the first person who set out the contents and inner logic of the Pauline

Epistles in a way that has commanded general assent ever since. Despite his quirks and mistakes here and there, he can still be read as an introduction to this key part of the New Testament. His style is usually clear and straightforward, something that can't always be said of modern commentators on the same texts.

Further, Ambrosiaster had a firm grasp of the theological and pastoral implications of Paul's epistles. His approach to them is a model for us today and reminds us that we have to look beyond the historical circumstances those epistles were originally composed in and see in them a message of salvation through faith in Christ that is as compelling now as it was then.

Ambrosiaster reminds us that God gives his gifts to humble people who may be unknown to the wider world but who are nevertheless used to edify the church. We cannot identify him among the great men of his time, but we can know where his heart lay and resonate with his love for Christ and for his people. In the end, that is what counts, and that is what we find in him.

• REFLECTION QUESTIONS •

1. How much are we able to guess about the life and career of an anonymous writer like Ambrosiaster? How important is his identity to our understanding of what he wrote?

2. Is it possible to find one central idea in Paul's letters, or are there several different themes that come out according to the circumstances in which particular letters were written?

• FURTHER READING •

Translated Texts of Ambrosiaster

Bray, Gerald L., ed. and trans. *Commentaries on Galatians–Philemon.* By Ambrosiaster. InterVarsity Press, 2009.

Bray, Gerald L., ed. and trans. *Commentaries on Romans and 1–2 Corinthians.* By Ambrosiaster. InterVarsity Press, 2009.

Studies

Lunn-Rockliffe, Sophie. *Ambrosiaster's Political Theology.* Oxford University Press, 2007.

Souter, Alexander. *A Study of Ambrosiaster.* Cambridge University Press, 1907.

5

JOHN CHRYSOSTOM

(ca. AD 349–407)

Who He Was

John was born to a Christian family in Antioch around the year 349.[1] His father died when he was young, and he was brought up by his mother. He received an excellent classical education, but when he was eighteen, he abandoned his studies and adopted a strict monastic way of life. He was baptized about this time and found refuge with a hermit. After four years in the hermit's cave, John branched out on his own. For two years he practiced the most extreme self-denial, fasting to the point where he did considerable damage to his health. In the end it was too much for him, and he returned to Antioch.

In 381 John was ordained a deacon, and five years later he was made a priest. For the next eleven years, he preached regularly in the city's main church. His most famous sermons were delivered during those years, and he developed an expository style of preaching, working his way through Genesis, Isaiah, and the Psalms in the Old Testament, as well as Matthew, John, and the Pauline Epistles (including Hebrews) in the New.

John's reputation spread, and in 397 he was elected patriarch of Constantinople. It turned out to be an unfortunate choice. Constantinople was a hotbed of corruption and political intrigue, and John condemned the moral laxity of the city and its church. By deposing unworthy clergy, he made enemies who were determined to get rid of him, and his denunciations of the imperial court's luxury earned him no friends there either. The empress Eudoxia turned against him, convinced by John's enemies that his criticisms were directed at her.

John also faced problems caused by the rivalry between Antioch and Alexandria. When Theophilus of Alexandria was summoned to Constantinople to answer charges leveled against him, the trial was presided over by John, and Theophilus believed that the whole affair had been instigated by him. Seeking revenge, Theophilus summoned a meeting of thirty-six bishops, twenty-nine of whom were Egyptians like himself, in order to try John on a series of trumped-up charges. The strategy worked, and John was deposed in August of 403.

He was expelled from the capital but was recalled the very next day when riots broke out in the city. John was restored to his office, but two months later he was again accused of attacking the empress, and this time the accusation stuck. The emperor Arcadius ordered John to retire, but John refused, and trouble soon followed. When the army tried to expel him from his church, the congregation resisted, with some loss of life. The situation became intolerable, and on June 9, 404, five days after Pentecost, John was forced to leave the city. He was exiled to the Armenian town of Cucusus (now Göksun in south central Turkey), where he lived for the next three years.

Cucusus was not far from Antioch, and his former parishioners were soon visiting him there, along with some dedicated followers from Constantinople. Moreover, Cucusus was subject to periodic raids by the mountain men of nearby Isauria, and John had to flee from them at least once during his stay there. The support he received from both Antioch and Constantinople alarmed John's enemies, who had the emperor banish him to Pityus (now Pitsunda in the Abkhazian region of Georgia). Forced to go there on foot and exposed to the hardships of bad weather and a semidesert terrain, John never made it to his destination. On September 14, 407, he died in Comana Pontica, a city that is now in ruins near modern Tokat, about halfway between Cucusus and the Black Sea.

John's death came to be seen as a martyrdom, and his fame spread. A century later, he became known as *Chrysostomos* ("golden-mouthed") because of his gift for preaching. The Roman church broke off relations with Constantinople because of what happened to John, and it was not until the wrong done to him was put right that relations between the two largest churches of the Christian world were restored. Thirty years after he passed away, John's remains were brought back to Constantinople, and Emperor Theodosius II (408–450), the son of Arcadius and Eudoxia, publicly begged forgiveness for his parents' sin in opposing John's ministry. In later times, John became the best loved of all the Greek fathers of the church, and his extensive legacy has been preserved almost intact. The simplicity of his life, the sincerity of his faith, and the sufferings he was unjustly forced to endure all combined to enhance his reputation, which was particularly strong among the Protestant Reformers of the sixteenth century, who regarded him as a model Christian leader.

How Chrysostom Read the Bible

John taught that God spoke to people by what he called "accommodation," a technique made necessary by the fundamental divide between the infinite Creator and the finite creation.[2] As John saw it, God reaches out to us by choosing words and pictures to represent something of himself in a way that we can understand. The obvious example of this is that he tells us that he is our Father, borrowing a human concept to explain something that is true of him. Of course, as John and all his contemporaries insisted, this is an analogy that should not be pressed too far—there is no divine mother, and we do not share the same being with God the way we do our human parents. Even so, there is a relationship between us that can be compared to the relationship that a human father has with his children. God cares for us, provides for us, and makes us coworkers with him, so we are not wrong to think of him in that way.

In the Old Testament, God had to speak to the Hebrews as children, telling stories and establishing ritual practices that were not true in themselves but pointed to a higher reality that was eventually revealed in Christ. For example, the people were commanded to sacrifice a lamb for their sins, even though the blood of an animal could never atone for the misdeeds of human beings. The apostle Paul used pictures to make his points, John claimed, because many of the people to whom he preached were incapable of understanding the straightforward reality of the gospel. An example that he gave is the way in which Paul "became like a Jew to gain the Jews" (1 Cor. 9:20 NET). Christianity was a replacement for Judaism, the grown-up version, if you like, of what had been revealed in a childlike way in the Old Testament. In John's eyes, Paul was not really a Jew and he did not advocate keeping the law of Moses—rather the opposite—but in order to make contact with those for whom Moses was the primary spiritual authority, he was prepared to adopt Jewish ways so he would be accepted by those he wanted to preach to.[3] Paul was always prepared to adapt his behavior in ways that would make it easier for him to communicate his message, as long as the gospel itself was not compromised.

Chrysostom and the Jews

It was this consideration that led Paul to circumcise Timothy, even though he did not believe that circumcision was of any spiritual value.⁴ So far, the modern reader can follow John without difficulty. But John went on to say that by circumcising Timothy, Paul was deliberately deceiving the Jews in order to gain their confidence. Once he had obtained that, said John, Paul set about demolishing the very thing he had used to appeal to them. John actually called this "deception," and what is more, he commended it to Christians as a perfectly proper way to behave. As we would say today, "The end justifies the means." But does it? At this point most modern readers might feel uncomfortable, even if they agree with John that Paul had Timothy circumcised for pragmatic reasons and that he had no desire to make circumcision compulsory for Christians. But we would almost certainly deny that this accommodation to Jewish sensitivities was a form of deception because we would not accept that circumcision is wrong—merely unnecessary. Jewish Christians can keep aspects of the Mosaic law if they want to, but they are not obliged to do so and can't force others to observe their particular customs.

To understand the significance of this, we need only look to the advice Paul gave to Christians who had to face weaker believers (almost certainly Jews) who could not in good conscience eat meat that had been sacrificed to idols. Paul's approach to them was essentially pragmatic: There is no need for Christians to eat such meat, he said, and if it offends some people, it is better not to do it. Paul's advice in that situation was not intended to deceive anyone, and there is no suggestion that he was hoping to soften up the recalcitrant Jews by accommodating himself to their preferences merely in order to break them down. His concern was not to get hung up on nonessentials that would take people away from the Christ who had died for them.

But John went further than that. He even traced Paul's pastoral practice back to the teaching of Jesus, who told his disciples that they would become "fishers of men" (Matt. 4:19). As John saw it, the disciples treated their fellow Jews like fish and regarded their message as a hook to ensnare them. Just as real fishermen are patient and wait for the hook to take hold, so the preachers of the gospel persevered with the more obstinate Jews, bowing to their traditions when necessary, until such time as the hook could no longer be removed. At that point, so John claimed, the Jews would realize that there was no going back to their former ways and would surrender to the truth of the gospel instead.[5]

Adapting the Message to the Audience

What should we make of this? We can agree with John that it is right to approach the task of evangelism with sensitivity and patience, but we may recoil from his assertion that this is a form of deception and cannot accept that such behavior is ever justifiable. To our minds, the disciples of Jesus were not trying to trick Jews into accepting the gospel message but merely trying to avoid unnecessary offense that would make it impossible for them to hear it. In coming to terms with John on this point, we have to recognize that he was openly anti-Jewish and had very little time for the so-called weaker brethren who resisted the truth in the name of their ancient traditions. If Paul accommodated himself to them, it was only to make them see things differently—in the light of Christ. As John saw it, as believers progressed from the basics of the gospel to its deeper principles, they would be transformed by the power of the Holy Spirit and abandon beliefs and practices that revealed a childish and immature faith. If they failed to do that, they were not growing in the grace of God and were not true believers at all. To Chrysostom, this was the fundamental problem with the Jews. They had a revelation suitable to spiritual infants but refused to give it up when a mature, adult faith was revealed in Christ. This refusal showed that they were not true believers, because if they were, they would have responded to the call of the Messiah in the way that Simeon, Anna, and the disciples of Jesus had done.

One feature of accommodation, as John saw it, was its precision. This seems strange at first because no analogy is perfect and it is hard to see how it could be precise or exact. But what John meant was that in his revelation, God established specific rules that were quite exact in their formulation and that illustrated what he meant by the principles that reflected his character. For example, we are told that God is love. But what does that mean? As John saw it, it means that we must not kill, steal, or commit adultery—these are the practical ways that demonstrate what the love of God is. Christian truth is not just a set of principles; it is also a program for everyday life. We cannot become like God in his essence, but by the power of the Holy Spirit, we can act as God would act in particular circumstances. God loved the world, not by giving it a philosophy to live by, but by sending his Son to die for our salvation. We, too, are crucified with Christ—united with him in his death and born again with him in his resurrection so that we can now walk in newness of life.

Living the Christian Life

John had a very high view of the Christian life. Origen did not think that it was possible for ordinary people to attain the high spiritual standards demanded of true believers and was content to accept that there would always be different levels of spirituality in the church, but John disagreed. He did not believe that being filled with the Holy Spirit was the preserve of a specially gifted elite, but the inheritance of every Christian. That, of course, merely intensified the need he felt to expound what the Christian life was and how it should be lived, making his interpretation of the Bible in many respects more down-to-earth and practical than Origen's had been. It is important to understand this, because the Greek-speaking world was very much under the spell of Origen in John's time, and what he had said was generally accepted as definitive. But Origen's propensity for allegory was coming into question in John's time and being rejected by many because it often seemed fanciful. John was among those who had doubts about Origen's allegorizing, and he preferred the literal sense of the text wherever he could. He did not attempt to explain difficulties away but interpreted them as having a deeper meaning alongside what they said on the surface—the material and the spiritual went together in Scripture, with the former pointing the way to the latter without being interpreted out of existence.

This approach to the Bible corresponded to John's doctrine of Christ, whom he saw as having two natures (one divine and the other human) that were united to such an extent that his human nature never did anything that might conflict with the divine. In particular, Jesus was never ignorant of anything because he was God incarnate, nor was his will distinguishable from that of the Father, despite what he said in the garden of Gethsemane.[6] John did not live to see the struggle to define the relationship between the two natures of the incarnate Christ, and he has been claimed by subsequent generations on both sides as one of their supporters. It is impossible to decide this question one way or the other. We can only say that John was a prime example of someone who lived before a particular theological controversy broke out and who now appears to have straddled what would later become a divide.

What we can say is that John believed that Jesus Christ was God in human flesh, that everything he thought, said, or did was essentially divine and that no other human being could be like him in that way. We can never be what Jesus was (and in his resurrection life, still is), but by the indwelling presence of his Holy Spirit, we can imitate him, not in his miracles or teaching but in his manner of life. As Paul put it, "We have the mind of Christ" (1 Cor. 2:16). He exhorted the Corinthians to imitate him just as he imitated Christ (1 Cor. 11:1). In John's view, that meant above all reaching out to others and adjusting to their way of thinking in order to communicate the higher knowledge that comes with the gospel. Just as the Son became human in order to proclaim salvation to us, so Paul became all things to all people for the same reason, and we are called to do the same. The Bible is the blueprint for the life we are meant to lead, and the preacher is the one who has to adapt its message and apply its teaching to those for whom it is intended.

Relating the Old Testament to the New

Central to any preacher's approach to the Bible will be their understanding of how the Old Testament relates to the New and vice versa, and John was no exception to this. His preference for a literal over an allegorical reading of the Hebrew Bible meant that he had to explain this relationship in a way that took account of history, and he did so by means of what we would now call promise and fulfillment. More specifically, he used John 4:36–37 to illustrate his point. In those verses, Jesus was speaking about the link between the sower and the reaper in the harvest of souls. The reaper is the one who gathers them in, but the sower is glad of this, because their labor has borne fruit. As John saw it, the prophets of the Old Testament were the sowers and the apostles of the New were the reapers:

> The prophets sowed but did not reap; that was the work of the apostles. But even so, the prophets were not deprived of the pleasure and reward of their labors. They rejoice and are glad with us, even though they are not reaping with us. . . . I have kept you [Jesus told his disciples] for the work that is less difficult and gives greater joy, for sowing is hard and difficult. . . . Jesus was trying to prove that the Prophets wanted everyone to come to him. This was also the intention of the Law. . . . He also showed [his disciples] that he had sent the prophets, and that there is a very intimate connection between the New Testament and the Old.[7]

In following this principle when interpreting the Old Testament, John was doing no more than walking in the footsteps of Jesus, who used the Scriptures for the same purpose. Particularly interesting is that although John recognized that God had spoken to Israel by more direct means, he pointed out that Jesus did not do the same. For example, Jesus never mentioned the appearance of God to Moses on Mount Sinai, or any of the other Old Testament theophanies. John guessed that the main reason for Jesus's silence was that when those incidents had occurred, many of the people did not believe them or pay attention to what God was saying. The Scriptures were different in that respect. They were an objective witness to God's revelation that was available to everyone and that Jewish believers deliberately studied in order to discern God's will. At the same time, most people lacked the discernment they needed in order to understand what the Bible was really about. The fact that it bore witness to the future coming of Christ was not universally recognized because it was hidden below the surface of the text and had to be deduced by spiritual insight. As John explains, "When Christ referred the Jews to the Scriptures, he sent them not to a mere reading but to a search. . . . The sayings related to him required close attention, for they had been concealed from the beginning. . . . He therefore asked them to dig down with care in order to discover what lay in the depths below. These sayings were not on the surface, nor were they exposed to open view, but rather lay like buried treasure, hidden very deep."[8]

That they were required to do this was not simply an idea tossed up by Jesus, but something that was rooted in the very identity of Israel. This was why Jesus told the Jews that their human ancestor Abraham had looked forward to his coming, a saying that John interpreted as a reference to the crucifixion, which he saw foreshadowed in the sacrifice that God had first ordered (and then overruled) of his son Isaac.[9] Not surprisingly, it was in this same encounter that Jesus effectively called himself God by saying, "Before Abraham was, I am" (John 8:58). The revelation of Christ in the Scriptures was ultimately the self-revelation of God to his people, and it was in that combination that the will of God and the fulfillment of his promises to Israel were to be discerned.

John the Preacher

John wrote a few treatises on moral and pastoral subjects and has left us a fair amount of correspondence, but his reputation rests mainly on the large number of his sermons that have survived. A difficulty with reading sermons is that it is impossible to recapture the original atmosphere in which they were preached. John's use of gestures, his tone of voice, his sense of humor, his allusions to contemporary events that are unknown to us now—all of these are lost to the modern reader. Nor can we be sure to what extent the texts we have represent what he actually said. Some of them may have been reproduced verbatim in written form, but it is probable that most of them were edited, either by John himself or by a literary executor. It is also possible that some of the sermons were never actually preached but were prepared directly for publication, using a standard homiletic format. We must therefore be careful not to assume too much about his preaching style, which may have been somewhat different from what the surviving evidence suggests. At the same time, John's live presentation cannot have been so different from the texts as to make it unrecognizable. We can be fairly certain that his imprint is stamped on the surviving sermons to a degree that makes them authentically his, even if we cannot recapture his original delivery.

John's most important sermons are expository ones on different books of the Bible. He was not the only church leader who preached in that way, but he was a master of the genre whose sermons were preserved when those of most others were forgotten. From the Old Testament we have seventy-six sermons on Genesis, subdivided into two collections. The first consists of eight homilies on Genesis 1–3, with a ninth that ranges over the remaining chapters. The second collection covers the entire book, with much of the material from the first series repeated almost word for word. We also have fifty-eight sermons on selected psalms and a complete series on Isaiah that survives only in an Armenian translation.[10] In addition to that, there are isolated sermons on Hannah, the mother of Samuel; on David and Saul; and on Elijah, along with extensive fragments of homilies on Job, Proverbs, Jeremiah, and Daniel.

From the New Testament, John has left us the first complete commentary on Matthew, which he covered in ninety sermons, and eighty-eight on the Gospel of John. He also produced fifty-five sermons on Acts, the only commentary on that book to have survived from ancient times, as well as a collection of 244 sermons on the Pauline Epistles, including Hebrews.[11] Most of these were delivered in Antioch, though the seventy-seven homilies on Philippians, Colossians, 1 and 2 Thessalonians, and Hebrews date from his time in Constantinople, as does the series on Acts. There are also a number of stand-alone sermons on particular passages, many of them tied to events in the life of Jesus that are commemorated in the liturgical year.

John never quoted Ruth or the short epistles of 2 and 3 John, and there are other books that he mentioned only once (Ezra, Esther) or twice (Nahum), but this seems to be accidental and does not indicate that he rejected their canonicity. John also accepted the Old Testament Apocrypha as Scripture, but he seldom used it. There are only three sermons on 1 and 2 Maccabees, for example, and a few quotations from other apocryphal books elsewhere. Like most of the church fathers, John accepted the Apocrypha as Scripture because it was part of the Greek Old Testament (Septuagint), but he had little use for it in practice and never preached on it systematically.

A number of John's sermons for preparing candidates for baptism have survived, as have occasional pieces composed to celebrate various liturgical feasts or to honor the memory of great saints and martyrs. Especially notable among these are seven sermons in praise of the apostle Paul, whom John admired and with whom he felt a particular kinship, perhaps because they were similar personalities.[12] Occasionally John stepped directly into the political arena, as when he preached a series of twenty-one sermons dealing with the destruction of the imperial statues by an Antiochene mob in 387. The emperor threatened to destroy the city in retaliation, but the intercession of Bishop Flavian persuaded him to show mercy. John's interventions were evenhanded. He deplored the emperor's thirst for vengeance and prayed that it might be stayed (as it was), but he also castigated the Antiochenes for their behavior, which had brought condemnation down on them.

To understand John's preaching, we have to consider what his intellectual background was and what he was trying to communicate to his congregations. All forms of literature are products of their time, and it is only if they can speak not just to the original hearers but also to the second and third generations that read them that they are likely to survive beyond the circumstances in which they were produced. If this is true of books, it is even more true of speeches, and sermons are a particularly focused form of speech.

Preachers do not necessarily look beyond their immediate congregations, but even if they do, they know that they must first persuade the people sitting in front of them of both the truth and the importance of what they have to say. That John's sermons have survived is an impressive testament to their worth, but even so, modern readers will inevitably find it difficult to enter fully into the spirit of his preaching. Today we live in an audiovisual world in which the spoken word is reduced to a minimum. Tweets and sound bites have replaced lectures and speeches, and for most people, a twenty-minute sermon is the most extended form of address that they are likely to hear on a regular basis. To make things even more difficult for the modern preacher, congregations are not trained to listen and absorb what they hear, so they are easily distracted or bored.

Teaching Everybody in the Congregation

Preachers nowadays usually have no training in rhetoric and have to learn from experience what communicates well to their congregations and what does not. John Chrysostom lived in a different world. In his time, oratory was highly prized, people were generally attentive to what they heard, and speakers were taught how to use their voice to best effect. Not everyone succeeded to the same degree, of course, but expectations were great and standards high. John inherited a long tradition of public speaking that went back to ancient Greece, and in particular to the great Athenian orator Demosthenes (mid-fourth century BC). Demosthenes was not just an ideal from the distant past but a model that John and his contemporaries were expected to imitate. In this endeavor he was universally acknowledged to have been one of the most successful, managing to produce a form of words so pure in its classical style that it could have come from seven centuries before his time. The amazing thing is that John achieved this without sounding stilted or archaic. Where others indulged in high-flown rhetoric, he kept everything simple and straightforward, recognizing that most people were put off by technical theological jargon that they could not understand. In modern times that approach has often been seen as lowbrow, but in reality he had mastered the essence of the classical style, which was to present complex ideas in a simple way that spoke to the educated and uneducated alike.

John believed that this was essential because the church included every class of society. One of the failings of classical Greek culture is that it was elitist. Schools of philosophy gathered around men like Plato and Aristotle, but while these disciples imbibed and developed their master's ideas, they paid little heed to the needs of ordinary people. The philosophers of John's day spoke to nobody but themselves, and too many of his fellow Christians were tempted to follow suit.[13] John resisted this trend, with the result that he achieved fame, not just as a theologian but also as a popular communicator who made Christianity comprehensible to a generation of people who, in many cases, were hearing it for the first time.

In sharp contrast to the elitism of classical Greek culture, the Christian church was a fellowship that embraced all types and conditions of humanity—rich and poor, Greek and "barbarian," male and female, young and old—everyone. The pagan philosopher could address a chosen few, but the Christian preacher had to speak to the whole range of their hearers, bringing God's Word to bear on intellectuals and nonintellectuals alike. It did not matter to John if a few highly educated snobs looked down on divine revelation as uncouth and simplistic. What he cared about was that it could be intelligible to all because it was intended for all, and as Scripture itself reminds us, it is often the poor and apparently foolish who shame the wise by their understanding of the deep things of God.[14]

John's calling to reach the full range of humanity was fortified by yet another basic principle of Christian belief. The philosophers had striven to achieve an intellectual synthesis that, by definition, was liable to be understood only by those who were capable of stretching their minds to absorb it. But the Christian God was unfathomable by even the cleverest intellect. Christian belief was the fruit not of academic labor but of spiritual awakening, and that awakening could come to the humblest and most unlikely people. Speaking of the apostle John, Chrysostom said:

> This completely ignorant man, who never went to school either before or after becoming a disciple of Christ—let us see what he says and what he talks to us about. Is it about things in the fields? Or about things in rivers? Or about the fish trade? We might expect that sort of thing from a fisherman, but that is not what we get. Not at all! Instead, we hear about the things of heaven, things that nobody ever found out before he revealed them. . . . Is this natural for a fisherman? Do orators speak this way? What about sophists and philosophers, or those who are trained in pagan wisdom? No. The human mind is simply incapable of philosophizing on the nature of heaven and what belongs to it.[15]

Spiritual awakening is the gift of God working through his Holy Spirit in the life of the church. As the apostle Paul explained to the Corinthians, there are different callings and ministries, but the same Spirit is present in all who believe. Like most people in the early church, John thought that the gift of the Spirit was given in baptism, but while modern readers might find this understanding too simplistic, Christians today will agree with him that it is only by the Spirit of God at work in our hearts that we can come to understand the gospel of Christ and take it into our lives.[16]

The fact that the church embraces all sorts of people means that its ministers must also serve them as fully and as impartially as possible. For John this meant giving special consideration to the poor, the socially outcast, and those who had been victimized by society for one reason or another. But it also meant castigating the wealthy and powerful, who were liable to abuse their standing and ignore the needs of those less fortunate than themselves. John believed that every household should reflect Christian values, with the weak being supported by the strong and with everyone learning the basic principles of Christian living by practicing them on a daily basis. The role of the pastor was to edify the church, by both teaching and example. John's model for this was the apostle Paul, whom he saw as the supreme expounder of the Christian life. Indeed, it perhaps is not too much to say that John regarded Paul much in the way that Paul regarded Jesus—as an example to imitate as far as possible in every situation and relationship.

This comes out clearly in the two sermons that he devoted to the list of people in Romans 16. Whereas many modern commentators see this chapter as an appendix to the epistle, even to the point of suggesting that it may not have belonged to the original text, for John it was central to the apostle's message. What he impressed on his hearers was that Paul was writing not just to the church but to particular people within it who mattered to him personally. This was the model that John himself tried to follow. Like Paul, he was a pastor at heart, and his preaching was tailored accordingly.

Salvation Made Available to Everyone

John demonstrated that the Bible is above all a message of salvation in Christ addressed to people everywhere. He did not read the text as a historical document but as a call to repentance and to new life in the kingdom of God. The Bible speaks today with the same power as it had when it was first written, and John is a witness to that. He knew that powerful preaching is used by God to change hearts and lives, and that is what he saw as his calling. He was not an ivory-tower theologian but a hands-on pastor who gave all he had for the conversion of his hearers to Christ.

He believed that he was called to preach the whole counsel of God. He had his favorite books—the Pauline Epistles—but that did not stop him from expounding other parts of Scripture, including the Gospels and the Old Testament. He did not live long enough to cover everything, but he ranged far and wide in the time that was given to him, and his legacy lives on.

John never compromised or tailored his message to suit particular groups. To him, the rich and powerful were as much in need of salvation as anyone else, and he spoke to everybody without fear and treated them equally. Nor did he talk down to his hearers. His sermons were models of oratory that carried conviction. Today we live in a time that has largely forgotten the power of the long-form spoken word, and John reminds us that it is worth spending time learning how to speak in a convincing and memorable way if we want to get our message across.

And yet John also reminds us of the truth of what Jesus said in Matthew 5:10–11: Faithful preaching will arouse opposition and may even lead to persecution, but what God requires of us is loyalty and obedience to him. John excelled at that, but he paid a price for it too. John shows us that sacrifice for the sake of Christ is never in vain, nor do the wicked who oppose the gospel succeed in the long term. His sermons have survived and are still being read today, while his enemies have been forgotten. Even a few years after his death, his reputation for holiness was such that the son of his imperial persecutors was forced to atone for his parents' sin, and John was honored more after his death than he had been during his lifetime. We may be called to suffer for Christ and die without seeing the fruits of our labors, but God will not forget us, and in his good time he will demonstrate to the world that true glory and honor belong to his good and faithful servants.

● REFLECTION QUESTIONS ●

1. Is expository preaching the best way to communicate the Word of God to the church? What should the balance be between doctrinal instruction and pastoral application?
2. How should a preacher react if their message arouses opposition? Is suffering for the truth an almost inevitable consequence of faithful preaching?

● FURTHER READING ●

Translated Texts of John Chrysostom

Goggin, Thomas Aquinas, trans. *Commentary on Saint John the Apostle and Evangelist*. 2 vols. By John Chrysostom. Fathers of the Church, 1957–1960.

Hill, Robert C., trans. *Homilies on Genesis*. 3 vols. By John Chrysostom. Catholic University of America Press, 1986.

Hill, Robert C., trans. *Saint John Chrysostom's Old Testament Homilies*. By John Chrysostom. Holy Cross Orthodox Press, 2003.

Schaff, Philip, and Henry Wace, eds. *Nicene and Post-Nicene Fathers*, series 1. Vols. 9–14. By John Chrysostom. Hendrickson, 1994.

Studies

Bray, Gerald L. *Preaching the Word with John Chrysostom*. Lexham Press, 2020.

Kelly, J. N. D. *Golden Mouth: The Story of John Chrysostom—Ascetic, Preacher, Bishop*. Baker, 1995.

Mayer, Wendy, and Pauline Allen. *John Chrysostom*. Routledge, 2000.

Mitchell, Margaret M. *The Heavenly Trumpet: John Chrysostom and the Art of Pauline Interpretation*. Westminster John Knox Press, 2002. Originally published in 2000 by Mohr Siebeck.

Rylaarsdam, David. *John Chrysostom on Divine Pedagogy: The Coherence of His Theology and Preaching*. Oxford University Press, 2014.

6

THEODORE
OF MOPSUESTIA

(ca. AD 350–428)

Who He Was

Theodore of Mopsuestia was born at Antioch around the same time as John Chrysostom, and both men studied under the same teachers there. They became good friends, and it was John who persuaded Theodore to enter a monastery, probably around 370. But Theodore was not called to a celibate way of life, and before long he married and became a lawyer. John, however, refused to give up and pleaded with his friend to reconsider. His powers of persuasion were such that Theodore returned to the monastery, and in 383 he was ordained a priest. We do not know what happened to his wife, but Theodore almost certainly did not divorce or abandon her, since that was forbidden by the church. She may have died, or perhaps the couple entered a spiritual marriage, a form of separation that permitted each partner to pursue a consecrated life of abstinence. In 392 he was elected bishop of Mopsuestia, a small town not far from Tarsus, and ministered there until his death in 428. During his lifetime he was widely acclaimed for his learning and for his theological orthodoxy, but after his death his reputation suffered, and in 553 he was posthumously condemned as a heretic and his writings were mostly destroyed or forgotten.

Theodore's career stands in sharp contrast to that of his friend John Chrysostom. Whereas John was a highflier who got into trouble and was only honored after he had passed away, Theodore led a quiet life and wasn't condemned until long after his death. As a result, it is John who is well-known today, whereas Theodore is relatively neglected. Modern scholars have appreciated him for what they see as his remarkably modern approach to the Scriptures, and some have regarded him as the victim of ancient prejudice. But those who interpret him in that light are usually unsympathetic to the church fathers in general, and so they have done little to restore Theodore to a place of honor. His rehabilitation has occasionally been attempted by those who recognize that his condemnation was unjust, but the weight of tradition and the difficulty of recovering his teaching have conspired to limit the amount of interest shown in him. But Theodore's work is worth reconsidering to the extent that it is available to us, and his importance for the life of the early church cannot be denied, however problematic later generations found him.

The Identity of Jesus Christ

What was it that led to Theodore's eventual fall from grace? To understand this, we have to look at the theological controversies that were raging in the late fourth and early fifth centuries, which Theodore himself largely stayed away from. He supported the condemnation of Arianism by the First Council of Constantinople in 381, although he was not in attendance. That council established what the orthodox doctrine of the Trinity would be, but it left other questions open. The most important of these concerned the identity of the incarnate Christ. After 381 everyone agreed that Jesus of Nazareth was the Son of God, equal to the Father and the Holy Spirit and sharing in their common mind and will. This was their common divine nature. But only one of these three became human—the Son.

The classic exposition of this doctrine was written by Athanasius (ca. 296–373), bishop of Alexandria from 328 and staunch defender of the First Council of Nicaea. Athanasius was fully orthodox, but on the humanity of Christ he was somewhat vague. He accepted that Jesus had a human soul (which included the mind and the will) but thought that it operated in conjunction with his divine nature, so that for practical purposes the two could hardly be distinguished. The sense that the incarnate Son of God did not need these things, because as God he had a mind and will already, was picked up by Athanasius's disciple Apollinaris, who took his master's approach to what he regarded as its logical conclusion. To him, the incarnate Christ was the Son of God encased in human flesh but not a human being in the same sense that we are. In 381, this view was condemned at the First Council of Constantinople, but no alternative to it was proposed.

In reaction to Apollinaris, Diodore of Tarsus, who was the leading theologian at Antioch, insisted that Jesus was a full human being—united with the Son of God, to be sure, but not lacking in anything necessary to humanity. The reason for that was that if Jesus had not been fully human, he could not have taken our place on the cross or died to pay the price of our sins. As Diodore and his followers understood it, sin is the fault of the soul, not of the inert flesh, and if Jesus did not have a human soul, he could not have been a substitute for us. The problem thus became one of defining what "humanity" is and how it can be applied to Christ. Everybody agreed that Jesus had been born to a virgin, who had conceived by the intervention of the Holy Spirit, but was the embryo in her womb a viable human being? In other words, would it have become the man Jesus of Nazareth, even if he had not been the eternal Son of God? The question was complicated because in popular devotion Mary was known as the *Theotokos* ("God-bearer"). Did this imply that she was the "Mother of God," and if so, in what sense?

Diodore and his followers were uncomfortable with the term *Theotokos*, because to them it suggested that Mary somehow gave birth to the divine nature (divinity) in her womb, which was clearly impossible. Mary was the mother of the human Jesus of Nazareth, not of the eternal Son of God, though as a result of the work of the Holy Spirit the Son was conjoined with the human embryo in her womb. The baby Jesus was therefore a conjunction of God and human, because both his divine and his human identity remained intact and distinct from each other. As the Son of God, Jesus was one of the three divine *hypostases* of the Trinity, so that was no problem. But as the son of Mary, was he a human *hypostasis* as well? That question had never really been asked before. To put it a different way, all human beings share a common nature—humanity—that is manifested in a particular identity, which constitutes our individual human *hypostasis*. Did Jesus of Nazareth have what we have in this respect, and if he did not, was he a real human being in the same sense that we are? The answer given by Diodore and accepted by Theodore was that Jesus did indeed have a human *hypostasis* in addition to his divine one, but precisely how they were united to each other in a single being was not explained.

The great problem with this was that it failed to identify the agent of the incarnation. Was it the *hypostasis* of the Son who entered the womb of Mary and took the elements of human nature on himself, or was Jesus Christ some kind of union between two distinct *hypostases* that could be undone without destroying either of them? When the disciples spoke to Jesus, were they speaking to God, to a human, or to both? When Jesus performed miracles, did he do so as God, as human, or as both? It was impossible to give a clear answer to questions like these, and the impression could be given that Jesus sometimes acted as God and sometimes as human, switching from one *hypostasis* to the other whenever he chose to do so. The matter came to a head when discussing the words of Jesus on the cross: "My God, my God, why have you forsaken me?" (Matt. 27:46). Which *hypostasis* said that, and what did he mean?

Neither Diodore nor Theodore answered that question directly, but it was later claimed that Nestorius, who may have been a pupil of Theodore's, did. Nestorius is supposed to have said that on the cross the Son of God abandoned the human Jesus of Nazareth to his fate. This was logical, because God cannot die, but humans can, and that is what Jesus did. Three days later the Son of God returned to the broken body of Jesus, restored the conjunction between them, and rose from the dead. Whether this was what Nestorius really taught may be doubted, especially as he denied it, but that is how Nestorianism was perceived and why Nestorius was condemned at the First Council of Ephesus in 431. By that time, Theodore was dead, and so we do not know what he would have said had he been present. But that is what the enemies of Nestorius claimed was his teaching, and the Nestorians believed that he had been following both Theodore of Mopsuestia and Diodore of Tarsus. To condemn Nestorius was therefore to imply that Theodore and Diodore ought to be condemned as well, even though nobody said that out loud.

This dispute went on for years and threatened the political unity of the Roman Empire. Emperor Justinian I (527–565), in an attempt to head off schism, decided to condemn what he regarded as Nestorianism. Seeking a wider consensus, Justinian summoned a council to meet at Constantinople in 553.[1] This Second Council of Constantinople somewhat reluctantly agreed to accept the emperor's decision, and so it was that Theodore, who had once been regarded as a pillar of orthodoxy, came to be denounced as a heretic. The Nestorians, most of whom were Syriac speakers living in the Persian Empire and therefore beyond Justinian's reach, continued to honor him, and many of his works survived in Syriac translations, some of which have been rediscovered and published in modern times. Nestorians still exist, though they are now very few in number and no longer possess theologians capable of defending their traditional position, so Theodore's condemnation remains frozen in time with no resolution in sight.

Whether Theodore's condemnation was justified is still debated, but nowadays it is generally agreed that it was at least unfair. By the time it happened, he was long dead. His views were filtered through the prism of later debates of which he knew nothing, and we can now recognize that many of the problems with his writings can be ascribed to the still imprecise definitions of key theological terms. But whatever opinion we may come to, the fact remains that lost manuscripts cannot be recovered, damaged reputations cannot easily be restored, and historic church divisions are likely to remain, especially now that they have developed traditions of their own that will not readily be given up. The scars of 553 are still visible, and we must bear them in mind as we try to figure out where Theodore belongs in the bigger picture of things, what exactly he believed, and why he is worthy of our attention today.

A Great Biblical Commentator

Theodore was a very prolific writer, and among other things, he produced highly original commentaries on most of the Bible. But the only work of his that is extant in Greek is his commentary on the twelve Minor Prophets (Hosea to Malachi). There is also a commentary on John's Gospel, which is complete in Syriac, though fragments of the original Greek text remain, as well as a commentary on the ten minor Pauline Epistles (Galatians to Philemon), which is extant in Latin, having been included by mistake with the works of Ambrose of Milan. Beyond that, it has been possible for modern scholars to reconstruct his commentaries on Genesis 1–3 (the *Hexaemeron*) and on Psalms 1–81 by piecing together fragments in both Greek and Syriac that have been preserved in other writings. There are a few fragments on the rest of the Pentateuch, Joshua, and Judges, as well as on Matthew's Gospel and the major Pauline Epistles (Romans, 1–2 Corinthians, Hebrews), but that is all that has survived. Of his other works, we have his *Catechetical Homilies*, which expound a version of the Creed of Nicaea and the Lord's Supper.[2] There are also fragments of a lost work titled *On the Incarnation*, which was discovered complete in Syriac in 1905 but was destroyed before it could be published.

The losses have been considerable, although it is not impossible that some of his works could yet turn up, most likely in Syriac translations that may have survived but so far have escaped undetected. On the other hand, there is a long tradition of Syriac commentaries that were based on Theodore's, often to the extent of being almost verbatim copies, and these give us a good picture of what he taught, even if we cannot be sure that they do not contain significant additions (or omissions!).[3] So although we would certainly like to have more, we are not entirely bereft of the information we need to form a coherent picture of Theodore's thought.

How Theodore Read the Bible

Theodore is known for an approach to the Bible that can justly be regarded as the exact opposite of Origen's. Whereas Origen used the literal sense of the text as a foundation for exploring its hidden meanings in different forms of allegory, Theodore eschewed allegory almost entirely. For him, the literal sense was the one that really mattered, and he usually read it with little imagination. This is especially evident in the Psalms, where he had no ear for poetry, and in parts of the New Testament, where he was ignorant of all

117

but the most obvious references to the fulfillment of prophecy in Christ. It was not that he was indifferent to prophecy in the Old Testament but that he regarded it as having been intended as a message for the prophet's contemporaries and essentially irrelevant to the distant future.

For example, he rejected the common understanding of Isaiah 53 as a prophecy of the sufferings of Christ and claimed that it had been fulfilled in Isaiah's own lifetime, though he could not say how.[4] Likewise, he understood Malachi 3:1 ("The Lord whom you seek will suddenly come to his temple") as a reference to the revolt of the Maccabees in the second century BC, when most other Christian commentators saw it as foretelling the coming of Christ.[5] He even claimed that the Song of Songs had been written by King Solomon in honor of his Egyptian bride and denied any connection to Christ and the church or the individual believer, an interpretation that by his time had become all but universal. According to the report presented to the Second Council of Constantinople in AD 553, this is what Theodore said:

> Although it was irksome for me to read the Song of Songs, since it is written neither in the prophetic genre nor in the tradition of history . . . I embarked on the reading with eager attentiveness, [but] I could not stop myself repeatedly yawning and dozing, bewitched by the book's nuptial banquet . . . [which] made Solomon vicious in the eyes of the Jews, as a transgressor of the ancestral laws that prohibit foreign marriages. . . . As a result, Solomon, in some distress because of his desire for his wife, and stung by reproaches at his transgression, composed a song in self-defense, in order to win his wife's favor by delighting her with songs specially written for her.[6]

Modern critics might praise Theodore for his purely secular interpretation, but it is not hard to see why the leaders of the church at the time would have been scandalized by his approach. Quite apart from anything else, how could a Christian bishop find the Word of God so boring? But note that despite his concern for historicity, Theodore mistakenly regarded Solomon as the author of the text, and even more mistakenly claimed that it was occasioned by his unpopular marriage to Pharaoh's daughter. In other words, his extreme literalism led him astray in his interpretation, and that was by no means a unique occurrence.

For example, Theodore believed that the Psalms were all written by David, even though he realized that many of them spoke of events long after David's time. He resolved this problem by claiming that David was a prophet, but he was very reluctant to see anything messianic about that. Theodore allowed that only four psalms (2, 8, 45, and 110) pointed toward Christ, and that was only because the New Testament said so explicitly, at least in the case of Psalms 2 and 110. Psalm 45, on the other hand, presented more of a challenge, especially in verse 8, which reads, "Your robes are all fragrant with myrrh and aloes and cassia." Theodore caved at this, allowing an allegorical interpretation for virtually the only time that we know of. He says, "By his robes he clearly meant the body, which was something put on from the outside, while inside there was his divinity, because of the indwelling [of the Son of God]."[7] Even more curiously, by saying this Theodore accidentally stumbled into what could easily be seen as Apollinarianism—the view that Christ's human body was a shell covering his divinity and not a real man—which, of course, was the exact opposite of what he believed.

Just as odd was Theodore's interpretation of Psalm 51. On the surface it appears to be a highly personal confession of sin by David himself and is usually associated with his remorse over the affair of Bathsheba, which would seem to have satisfied Theodore's criterion of historicity without further comment. But in fact, Theodore did not read the psalm that way at all. To him, the sin being confessed was not David's but Israel's, expressed not in David's time but during the exile in Babylon. In saying this, Theodore was following his master Diodore of Tarsus, who had said the same thing, but it is nevertheless a strange reading of the text.[8] Theodore was well aware that Psalm 51 has a title attributing it to David himself, but he disregarded that on the grounds that all the titles given to the Psalms had been added later and were pure guesswork on the part of editors who did not know what the original context was.[9] Theodore may have been devoted to the literal, historical reading of the Bible in principle, but as this example shows, it did not always work out that way in practice. What we often find is a curious mixture in which plausible interpretations occur alongside highly improbable ones, even though both claim to be historically accurate.

Understanding Old Testament Prophecy

Theodore was on surer ground in his interpretation of the Old Testament prophets. He stuck fairly rigidly to the principle that their prophecies were to be understood in relation to what for them was the foreseeable future and not to be read in a messianic sense. Thus he read Hosea 13:14 ("O Sheol, where is your sting?") as a reference to the Assyrians who were attacking Israel at that time, and not to Christ or to the resurrection on the last day, despite the fact that the apostle Paul quoted it in the latter sense.[10] He also read Micah 4:2 ("For out of Zion shall go forth the law") as a prophecy that the people would return from exile, and not as a foreshadowing of the coming of Christ, which was then the standard interpretation in the church. But even here, he occasionally got into difficulties and had to compromise. In Zechariah 9:9 ("Behold, your king is coming to you . . . humble and mounted on a donkey"), for example, he insisted that the "king" in question was Zerubbabel, despite the fact that Zerubbabel was never crowned as such. On the other hand, he was forced to admit that there was a secondary application to Jesus's triumphal entry into Jerusalem on Palm Sunday because the Gospels were too clear on that point for him to be able to ignore them.[11]

Jonah presented Theodore with particular difficulties. The story itself seemed historically improbable because, as Theodore remarks, the Ninevites "could never have believed in God on the basis of this remark alone, from a completely unknown foreigner threatening them with destruction and adding nothing further, not even letting the listeners know by whom he was sent. It is obvious that he must have mentioned God the Lord and that he had been sent by him [even though the text does not say so]."[12]

Theodore sensed that he had to add a plausible explanation to cover what would otherwise be extremely unlikely, but he was somewhat discomfited by the general strangeness of the book. He took refuge in the words of Jesus, who referred to Jonah as a sign, and writes, "It is obvious from the facts that he [God] chose to employ the blessed Jonah and do novel and extraordinary things, for the reason that he intended to present him as a type of the life of Christ the Lord, and so for this reason he [Jonah] was led on by such incredible novelty and proved worthy of belief, displaying in his own person a type of such a great reality."[13] Of course, what was "obvious" to Theodore might not appear that way to anybody else, but it was a solution to the problem created by his insistence that the prophecies should have a natural explanation, which in Jonah's case was hard to find.

It was very different with Hosea, whom God called to marry the prostitute Gomer.[14] This might seem to be quite "novel and extraordinary" to most people, but it did not bother Theodore in the slightest. On the contrary, he commented on it by mentioning another peculiar incident in Isaiah and explaining such things as follows:

> The fact that God had the prophets do a number of things that to most ordinary people seems improper, like ordering Isaiah to appear naked and barefoot in public,[15] clearly has the following explanation. Given that ordinary people like us normally do not pay much attention to words, but are startled when we are struck

by something new and unusual, it made sense for God . . . to have the prophets frequently do such things so that people would sit up and pay attention, and so come to understand and be taught to do their duty. This is why he told the prophet to marry a prostitute.[16]

Theodore was particularly adamant in insisting that nobody in the Old Testament knew anything about the Trinity, and so to read that doctrine into the text, as Hippolytus, Apollinaris, Eusebius, and Jerome had all done in their comments on the horses of various colors in Zechariah 1, was mistaken. In his mind, "It is obvious that none of those who lived before the coming of Christ the Lord knew of [God the] Father and [God the] Son. . . . The people before the coming of Christ the Lord were aware only of God and creation, identifying God as eternal in his being and the cause of everything, and creation as what he had brought into being from nothing."[17] Similarly, the people of the Old Testament had no inkling of the Holy Spirit, so that Joel 2:28, quoted by Peter on the day of Pentecost, did not apply to him as a distinct person of the Godhead.[18] Here Theodore was skating on the thinnest of ice, and it's easy to see why so many people objected to what they believed was far too narrow an interpretation of the prophet's message.

The Human Jesus and the Son of God

In his commentary on John's Gospel, and more generally in the New Testament, Theodore lost no opportunity to insist on the clear distinction between Jesus of Nazareth the human and Christ the Son of God. For example, when commenting on John 5:30, he writes, "[Jesus] then added, 'As I hear, I judge,' meaning, because of what the Word teaches me, I have the excellence of God the Word who dwells in me."[19] Similarly, on John 10:17 he says, "If, on the basis of his humanity, [Jesus] asserted that he has the power to lay down his soul and to take it up again, this is not at all surprising. . . . He has the power to do what is beyond his

[human] nature because of his union with God the Word. . . .
He also has the power to raise himself after his death because he
participates in this power on account of his union with God the
Word."[20] What does "union with God the Word" actually mean?
Can Theodore be understood to be saying that Jesus was a man
filled with the Son of God, who was nevertheless somebody else? It
is this kind of uncertainty that makes it so hard to decide whether
he was orthodox or not.

Finally, Theodore had to face the challenge of allegory, as this
was mentioned by the apostle Paul in Galatians 4:24, where he
compares Jews and Christians to Hagar and Sarah, the enslaved
concubine and the free wife of Abraham, respectively. Was Paul's
appeal to what he called allegory an open invitation to use that
method more generally to interpret the Scriptures? To that Theodore replied in no uncertain terms:

> Men who take great pains to falsify the sense of the divine Scrip-
> tures and to convert to their own ends all that is written in them
> actually fabricate foolish fables . . . and propose the name of *al-
> legory* to designate their folly, so taking false advantage of the words
> of the apostle in this passage. . . . The apostle does not abolish the
> historical sense of the passage nor does he do away with the events
> of the distant past, but he narrated those events just as they had
> taken place and made use of the historical sense according to his
> own understanding of it.[21]

In other words, Paul was using what we would now call typology and what Theodore would have known as *theoria* ("insight")
into historical events that had parallels in later times, but that
were in no way diminished by that. On the contrary, the fact
that history repeated itself, albeit in a somewhat different way,
was confirmation of the validity of the ancient witness and proof
that God had revealed himself to his ancient people just as much
as he was now revealing himself to their Christian descendants.

A Modern Man in Ancient Times?

Theodore is attractive to modern interpreters of Scripture because he rejected fanciful allegorical interpretations and did his best to establish biblical scholarship on the right exegetical principles. Even if he did not get everything right, many people think that his approach ought to guide our interpretation of Scripture today.

When it was necessary to challenge the reigning consensus of his day, Theodore did not hesitate to do so, and this independence of mind is also attractive to many people today. He did not elevate tradition to a place of authority that would effectively prevent fresh thought or serious research, and in that respect his affinity with modern commentators and theologians is obvious.

Theodore stands out as an example of someone who was unfairly treated by later generations that expected him to conform to their standards, of which he knew nothing. We often come across similar things today when great people of the past can be condemned for not sharing our values about things like slavery, gender equality, and so on. We cannot adopt their views, of course, but neither should we condemn them for not having been like us in every respect. We can still learn from people like Theodore, even if we disagree with them at times, and it is important for us to keep a sense of historical perspective when trying to evaluate their lives and careers.

● REFLECTION QUESTIONS ●

1. Is it right to condemn people for holding views that were unexceptional at the time but that came to be rejected centuries after their death?

2. Can a teacher be blamed when their pupils misunderstand their teachings and take them to extremes, even if it can be shown that those extremes were their logical consequence?

● FURTHER READING ●

Translated Texts of Theodore of Mopsuestia

Conti, Marco, trans. *Commentary on the Gospel of John*. By Theodore of Mopsuestia. InterVarsity Press, 2010.

Greer, Rowan, trans. *Commentary on the Minor Epistles of Paul*. By Theodore of Mopsuestia. Society of Biblical Literature Press, 2010.

Hill, Robert C., trans. *Commentary on Psalms 1–81*. By Theodore of Mopsuestia. Society of Biblical Literature Press, 2006.

Hill, Robert C., trans. *Commentary on the Twelve Prophets*. By Theodore of Mopsuestia. Catholic University of America Press, 2004.

Studies

Hill, Robert C. *Reading the Old Testament in Antioch*. Society of Biblical Literature Press, 2005.

McLeod, Frederick G. *The Roles of Christ's Humanity in Salvation: Insights from Theodore of Mopsuestia*. Catholic University of America Press, 2005.

McLeod, Frederick G. *Theodore of Mopsuestia*. Routledge, 2009.

Ondrey, Hauna T. *The Minor Prophets as Christian Scripture in the Commentaries of Theodore of Mopsuestia and Cyril of Alexandria*. Oxford University Press, 2018.

Sullivan, Francis A. *The Christology of Theodore of Mopsuestia*. Gregorian University Press, 1956.

Wallace-Hadrill, D. S. *Christian Antioch: A Study of Early Christian Thought in the East*. Cambridge University Press, 1982.

Zaharopoulos, Dimitri Z. *Theodore of Mopsuestia on the Bible: A Study of His Old Testament Exegesis*. Paulist Press, 1989.

7

JEROME

(ca. AD 347–419)

Who He Was

Jerome (or Hieronymus in Latin) was born about 347 in Stridon, a town of Dalmatia that cannot now be identified.[1] He was of Illyrian origin but thoroughly Latinized in culture and educated at the highest level the province he lived in could offer. That was not enough for an ambitious young man, however, and his parents sent him to Rome as soon as they could. There he received the best education available at the time and made important contacts that were to stand him in good stead later on. Sometime around 369 he was baptized while still in Rome, but shortly afterward he went to Trier, where he encountered the monastic way of life, which at that time was gaining popularity across the Roman world. He later returned home and lived for a while in the household of Bishop Valerian of Aquileia, along with some of his friends, including Rufinus, with whom he would later work on translations of Greek Christian literature, especially the works of Origen. Things did not work out for him in Aquileia, however, not least because he had a cantankerous character that would grow worse as he got older. When Evagrius of Antioch, one of his companions in Aquileia, went home in 373, Jerome and Rufinus followed him, a decision that was to affect the rest of Jerome's life.

Once he arrived in Syria, Jerome embarked on serious study of Greek and even of Hebrew, which made him almost unique among his contemporaries. He spent some time among hermits in the desert, but although he became aware of the theological controversies that were dividing the Eastern churches, he managed to stay out of them. It was during this time that he had a vision of himself being flogged before the judgment seat of Christ because he had devoted more time to the secular Latin classics than to Christian writings, and he vowed to change his habits, though, as his writings were to demonstrate, he was not very successful at that. To the end of his days he remained deeply attached to the great pagan Roman writers Virgil and Cicero, though he never mastered their Greek equivalents, despite claiming that he had.

After a few years in Syria, Jerome was ordained to the priesthood and became attached to Bishop Paulinus of Antioch, who was deeply involved in the controversies of the Eastern churches. That took him to Constantinople, where he met and befriended Gregory of Nazianzus. In 381 he was an observer at the council there that condemned both Arius and Apollinaris. Afterward he went on with Paulinus to Rome, where he spent the next few years. Jerome was always in need of wealthy patrons who could finance his various projects, and his stay in Rome was an important time for him to recruit them. He was particularly attractive to a number of aristocratic women who became his devoted followers, an unusual development that did not escape the censorious eyes of some church officials who eventually forced him to leave the city. It was during his time in Rome that Pope Damasus I approached him with the suggestion that he should edit the Latin Bible, which was circulating in a number of different versions that were causing confusion in the church. The reason for that is that no official translation existed. Latin-speaking Christians often produced versions of their own based on Greek, and this led to chaos because there was nobody to say which of them was better than the others.

Jerome agreed to undertake this task, and in a few years he had produced a version of the Gospels that would form the basis of a standardized Latin Bible. Over the years, other books followed, though it is not clear how much of the editing was the work of Jerome personally. In any case, he got the credit for the translation, which became what we call the Vulgate version of the Bible.[2] That translation soon displaced the others and remained the official text of the Roman Catholic church until the late twentieth century, when it was finally replaced by a modern critical edition.[3]

After the death of Damasus I in 384, Jerome was no longer welcome in Rome, and he made his way back to the East, accompanied this time by a retinue of followers, including some of the aristocratic ladies he had met in the capital. In 386 he established himself at Bethlehem, where he remained for the rest of his life. It was then that his writing career began in earnest, with a definite bias toward the Old Testament and Hebrew, which he believed needed attention more than the more familiar New Testament and Greek. He also maintained extensive correspondence with people all over the world, most notably with Augustine of Hippo, who managed to earn Jerome's respect despite their very different interests and personalities. The letters they exchanged have survived and give us a good picture of how the Bible was read and understood in the Latin-speaking world of the time. Jerome and Augustine might easily have clashed, but Augustine's humility in dealing with his older colleague prevented a serious falling out, and the emergence of the Pelagian controversy after 410 united them in a common cause.

Jerome never met Augustine, and their relationship was politely formal rather than warm, but that was a considerable achievement under the circumstances. Jerome was an irascible character and quarreled with many people over the course of his career, but the worst conflict came after 393 when he and his erstwhile friend Rufinus disagreed over the legacy of the long-dead Origen. Both men were caught up in a controversy about Origen's theological views, some of which, like his belief in the preexistence of souls, were widely regarded as heretical. Jerome distanced himself from Origen's eccentric theology and from his propensity for allegory, but Rufinus was more hesitant. Until about 393 both of them had been devoted disciples of Origen and had been planning a comprehensive series of translations of his writings into Latin. Rufinus carried on with that project, but Jerome became increasingly critical of it, which led to a bitter dispute between them that was never healed.

It has to be said that from most points of view, Rufinus comes out of that quarrel better than Jerome, who continued to value Origen's biblical exegesis and to borrow extensively from it even as he condemned the man himself. Rufinus, on the other hand, preferred to expunge certain passages of Origen when making his translations, claiming that the offending passages had been interpolated by Origen's enemies after his death. He was wrong about that, but his labors mean that we now have access to Origen, particularly to his great commentary on the Epistle to the Romans that would otherwise have perished almost completely.

Jerome's final years were unhappy ones. Old friends were either alienated or died, including some of his faithful female followers to whom he was attached. The demands on his skills as a translator and exegete continued to be heavy ones, and he was unable to respond to many of the requests he received for further commentaries on Scripture. The fall of Rome to the Goths in 410 sent shock waves around the empire, and Jerome was as deeply affected by the news as any other Roman. A few years later, the heretic Pelagius appeared in Jerusalem, having escaped the condemnation of his views in North Africa, and Jerome found himself in conflict with him. This turned serious in 416, when some of Pelagius's supporters burned Jerome's monasteries down. Recovery proved to be difficult, despite Pelagius's expulsion from the East in the following year. Jerome passed away on September 30, 419, an old and embittered man, as Augustine remarked when he heard the news.

Jerome's Writings

Like most of the church fathers, Jerome published a number of sermons and tracts on various subjects, but none of these are widely read today. His fame as an author rests on his biblical commentaries, which occupied most of his attention throughout his working life. That is not surprising, but Jerome's choice of books to comment on was unusual. His first effort was on the prophet Obadiah, but it was later superseded and is of little importance. His earliest commentary that survives intact was on Philemon, which he wrote at the behest of his friend Paula and her daughter Eustochium. These women wondered why such a short epistle should be in the New Testament and saw little value in it, but Jerome did not agree. He managed to show them that in fact Philemon is of profound theological significance and is fully deserving of its place in the canon of Scripture. The commentary appeared shortly after his arrival in Bethlehem, and it set off a chain of commentaries drawn from the writings of the apostle Paul.

Within a year, Jerome had produced commentaries on Galatians, Ephesians, and Titus, an odd collection by any standards.[4] We know that he regarded Ephesians as the best exposition of Paul's theology and that he used Titus as a kind of handbook to promote asceticism, but why he never went on to expound the rest of the Pauline corpus, as so many of his contemporaries did, remains something of a mystery. The best explanation is that he was not particularly interested in the New Testament from a scholarly point of view. He did eventually write a commentary on Matthew's Gospel in 398, but nothing more.

Jerome's main interest was always in the Old Testament, reflecting his fascination with Hebrew and his concern to make sure that his Latin translations reflected that, and not the Greek versions that were not always reliable. But here again, his choice of subjects was not typical. Most of the fathers wrote on the six days of creation, but although Jerome dabbled in Genesis, he never really got to grips with the Pentateuch. Nor was he particularly taken by the Historical Books, the Psalter, or the Wisdom Literature, despite his early foray into Ecclesiastes. His concentration was on the Prophets, and he was almost unique in the patristic period in that he produced detailed commentaries on all sixteen of them.

Prophecy was, of course, a controversial subject because it was not clear if and when it had been fulfilled. Christians generally believed that the prophecies were about the coming of Christ, but Theodore of Mopsuestia, a contemporary of Jerome's, disagreed, and Jews did not accept that either. For someone caught up with Hebrew, the Prophets were bound to pose a challenge, especially since Jerome was acutely aware that Jews would never accept Christ if they were not persuaded that the Prophets foretold him specifically.

It was in 393 that Jerome started his commentary project on the Prophets, covering Nahum, Micah, Zephaniah, Haggai, and Habakkuk—in that order. Why he chose to go about things in this way is unknown and is perhaps best ascribed to his innate eccentricity.[5] Unfortunately, the publication of these commentaries coincided with the outbreak of the Origenist controversy, which occupied his attention for several years. He did manage to complete Jonah and Obadiah in 396, and in them we can detect a certain hostility to Origen's theology, though it did not seriously affect his dependence on Origen's exegesis, which remained as strong as ever. He also managed to write on the ten visions of Isaiah, a work that was later incorporated into his longer commentary on the prophet, but after that there were several years of silence.

It was not until 406 that he was able to complete the series of the twelve Minor Prophets, but once again the order in which he treated them was peculiar. He started with Zechariah and went on from there to Malachi, Hosea, Joel, and Amos. We happen to know that he wrote to Didymus the Blind in Alexandria, asking him to pen something on Zechariah, which Didymus duly did. That commentary was lost until 1941, but when it was rediscovered, it became apparent that Jerome's commentary on the same prophet was so heavily dependent on Didymus that in places it amounted to little more than a translation. Since Didymus probably got most of his inspiration from Origen, it gives us yet another clue as to the nature of Jerome's reliance on him, but because Origen's commentary on Zechariah is lost, we cannot be sure about that.

Having finished the Minor Prophets, Jerome went on in short order to tackle the Major ones, hoping to complete the series before his death. Daniel appeared in 407, Isaiah in 408 or 409, Ezekiel in 411 to 414, and finally Jeremiah, which he began in 418 and left incomplete at his death, having reached only chapter 32. Yet again, the order in which he wrote them is odd and without clear explanation.

Despite his relative seclusion in Bethlehem from 386 onward, Jerome had a colorful and controversial life that earned him as many enemies as friends, but nobody could doubt his brilliance as a scholar and exegete. After his death, the unique quality of his work came to be increasingly recognized, and the Vulgate established itself as a monument of Latin literature whose beauty was appreciated for centuries afterward. But although Jerome triumphed in the end, the progress of his work and reputation was not uninterrupted, and in some cases it failed to leave a lasting imprint.

This is most notable in the Psalter, where Jerome's translation from the Hebrew never caught on. To this day, the Roman church has continued to use a version of the Psalms that is probably the one Jerome was initially asked to correct. Another version—based on Origen's *Hexapla* and canonized as the Gallican Psalter because it became the text of the Carolingian church in the eighth century—wormed its way into the Latin liturgy and even into the sixteenth-century revision of the Vulgate, and it was not replaced until modern times. Yet in spite of everything, the legend of Jerome as the great translator of the Bible persists to the present day, and he continues to be honored as much as for what he represents as for what he actually accomplished.

Jerome's commentaries continued to be read throughout the Middle Ages and were generally highly regarded, though Martin Luther was unimpressed by what Jerome had to say about Galatians, and his first lectures on that epistle, delivered in 1519, were highly critical of his illustrious predecessor. The nineteenth-century revival of interest in the church fathers, which led to widespread translations of their works, largely passed Jerome by. Biblical scholars did not make much of Jerome's writings, and they were often thought to be too long for the general public to read. The first modern English translation (of his commentary on the book of Daniel) did not appear until 1977, and it stood alone for the rest of the twentieth century. Then, all of a sudden, there was an upsurge of interest in Jerome's works, and between 2001 and 2017 the entire corpus appeared, making it possible for modern readers with no knowledge of Latin to access them for the first time. Whether that will lead to a renaissance of Jerome studies remains to be seen, but Jerome has been one of the great beneficiaries of the recent revival of interest in the writings of the church fathers, and there may be greater things yet to come.

How Jerome Read the Bible

There is no doubt that Jerome's modern reputation rests almost entirely on his ability as a translator. He was not asked to produce a new translation but merely to sort out the excessive number of existing ones, though trying to do that inevitably led him back to the Greek and from there to the original Hebrew of the Old Testament. He was convinced that any attempt to translate or expound that text had to be based on the Hebrew, which was virtually unknown in the church of his time. Even the New Testament writers frequently used the Septuagint when they quoted from the Hebrew Scriptures, so Jerome's convictions on this point went against Christian tradition and practice to a surprising degree. He persisted, however, with the result that his Latin version was closer to the original than it would otherwise have been. Unfortunately, his example was not followed until the sixteenth-century Reformation, and even then, the Roman Catholic Church, which continued to use Latin in its liturgy, rejected it. At the Council of Trent in 1546, Jerome's Vulgate was imposed as the official Catholic version of the Bible, and it remained so for more than four hundred years.

How familiar Jerome really was with the Hebrew Bible is a matter of debate, but the fact that he gave it priority over any translation is not. The Hebrew version that he used was almost identical to the Masoretic Text that is standard in Judaism today, but although he consulted with rabbis, it is apparent that much of what he wrote actually derived from Origen, his only Christian predecessor in Hebrew studies. Whatever we make of that, Jerome's principle was that the original text is what counts, and on that score he must be given the credit he is due. He could not ignore the Septuagint, of course, because it was the normal version used by the church, but although he had a generally low opinion of it, his willingness to include it among the possible witnesses to the original Hebrew text was more prescient than he imagined. Modern discoveries, notably of the Dead Sea Scrolls in 1947, have shown that the ancient Hebrew Bible was more varied than the Masoretic version would suggest, and some of the variations that the Masoretes either suppressed or did not know about have been preserved in the Septuagint translation. So the verdict of history must be that Jerome was wise to keep it as a resource, even though he did not know what its true value was.

Jerome also understood how difficult translation can be, and he wrestled with this when trying to find good Latin equivalents for both Hebrew and Greek phrases. The structure of Latin is very different from Hebrew and somewhat simpler than Greek, making word-for-word translation awkward or even impossible in many places. To resolve that difficulty, Jerome resorted to something not far from what we would now call dynamic equivalence, which means finding the right meaning being conveyed by the original, even if its exact words and phrasing cannot be reproduced in another language. A second-century Jew named Aquila had already produced an extremely literal translation of the Hebrew into Greek, but everybody agreed it was virtually unreadable, and Jerome knew he had to avoid that. At the same time, he also knew that biblical Greek had been shaped by Hebrew idiom in the course of translation and that Latin could be expected to experience something similar. It was knowing the difference between what was acceptable and what was not that was important, and in that Jerome excelled. As he writes in one of his letters, "We should always follow the rule that I have repeated so often, namely that where there is no difference in the meaning, we should translate idiomatically and use natural sounding language (*euphonia*)."[6]

Against the odds, Jerome managed to produce a Latin text that was not only elegant and meaningful but faithful to the spirit and message of the original, a feat that, as any translator knows, is not to be taken for granted! When the time came for his Latin to be replaced by the modern European languages, it was those translators, like Martin Luther for the German and William Tyndale for the English, who managed to achieve a similar result who are now honored as Jerome has always been—and for the same reason.

Getting Translation Right

Compared with Latin, both Hebrew and Greek have a way of loading many concepts into a single word, forcing the translator to choose the most appropriate one. For example, the Hebrew word *beit* is usually translated as "house" (*domus* in Latin), which could be called its basic meaning. But Jerome knew that sometimes *domus* was not appropriate, and he chose more precise Latin terms, like *aedes* (Amos 3:15), *armamentarium* (Isa. 22:8), *templum* (Mic. 3:12), or *cella* and *apotheca* (both in Isa. 39:2).[7] These words described different kinds of buildings and appeared to fit the various contexts better, even though Hebrew does not make such distinctions. Hebrew also has a way of repeating itself for the sake of emphasis, but when that happens, Jerome often omitted the repeat phrase, regarding it as awkward in Latin, where emphasis is normally expressed in other ways. Considering that both he and the Jews believed that every jot and tittle of the Hebrew text was inspired by God, and that Jesus had said that none of it would ever change, Jerome's freedom in this respect is truly remarkable.[8]

This freedom can sometimes seem surprising or even objectionable to us. A text that embarrassed Jerome was Galatians 5:12, where Paul exclaimed, "I wish those who unsettle you would castrate themselves!" (NRSVUE).[9] Even Jerome, who was not given to delicacy when it came to hurling insults at those he disagreed with, found this too much to take, and tried his best to explain it away, saying, "What Paul has said is not so much words of fury directed against enemies as words of love directed at God's churches. . . . Nor is it any wonder if the apostle, as a man still enclosed in a frail vessel, and one who sees the law in his own body taking him captive and leading him into the law of sin [Rom. 7:23], should have spoken like this once. For we observe such lapses frequently in holy men."[10]

When this commentary reached Augustine, he refused to believe that Paul could have made such a slip, especially since the apostle was writing under the inspiration of the Holy Spirit. But of course he could not erase Paul's offending words from the text, so he reinterpreted them by saying that "with very elegant ambiguity, Paul inserted a blessing under the appearance of a curse."[11]

And what was that blessing? The troublemakers were to castrate themselves in order to make themselves eunuchs for the kingdom of heaven, and that way they would no longer sow such carnal seed.[12] Jerome's explanation may be hard to take, but Augustine's is surely much worse!

Another embarrassment for Jerome occurred in Galatians 2:11, where Paul wrote, "But when Cephas [Peter] came to Antioch, I opposed him to his face, because he stood condemned." What had happened was that when Peter was in Antioch, he ignored Jewish food laws because they did not apply to the Gentiles he was with. But when a delegation from Jerusalem turned up, insisting that Gentile converts should be circumcised—that is to say that they should become Jews before becoming Christians—Peter was afraid of these Judaizers and stopped eating with the Gentiles. Paul regarded this as blatant hypocrisy and called Peter out on it, though to what effect we are not told.

Jerome treated this incident in two ways.[13] First, he pointed out that Peter had been cured of his anti-Gentile prejudices by the vision he had had before he went to visit the Gentile convert Cornelius in Caesarea Maritima, when God had told him not to call anyone common or unclean.[14] Then he went on to cite many passages of Scripture that proved that Paul also made accommodations to Jewish sensibilities, so he could not possibly have been objecting to Peter on those grounds.[15] His conclusion was that Peter was not condemned in Paul's eyes but in the eyes of the Gentile converts he was now shunning. The problem was that they did not understand that Peter was merely trying to win over Jews by accommodating himself to their sensitivities, as Paul regularly did!

Not surprisingly, Augustine found that interpretation hard to swallow, and he wrote to Jerome demanding that he recant.[16] Augustine believed that there was a fundamental theological disagreement between Paul and Peter, that Peter was wrong, that he accepted Paul's rebuke, and that he repented. Peter's greatness,

Augustine later claimed, lay not in his seniority to Paul as an apostle but in the humility he showed in accepting correction from a junior, perhaps echoing a parallel he would have seen between himself as the junior in relation to Jerome.[17] Augustine was right to dispute Jerome's interpretation, which he probably got from Origen and which went too far in saying that Peter was himself a Judaizer. Paul rebuked him not because of that but because Peter knew better and was not following his own convictions in this instance and causing distress in the church at Antioch. Jerome was correct in what he said about both Peter and Paul and their attitude toward Judaism, but here he missed the point and so ended up making excuses for both of them unnecessarily.

Jerome's forays into the New Testament are early examples of his commentary techniques, which developed over time. He paid serious attention to the literal sense, especially in his commentary on Matthew, where he treats everything as literal history, albeit with a spiritual dimension. The relationship between the literal and the spiritual meanings is fairly obvious in the Pauline Epistles and required relatively little explanation there or elsewhere in the New Testament. It was a different matter with the Old Testament, though, and it would be here that Jerome's expertise would be put to the test.

As with the New Testament, he gave the literal sense of the text pride of place in his exegesis, not least because it enabled him to demonstrate his Hebrew skills. Jerome knew that ancient Israelite culture gave great importance to the names of people and places. It was customary for the Jews to name their children prophetically, and so Jerome frequently explains what a person's name means so as to indicate what their role in Israel's history would be.[18] Place names, on the other hand, were usually given to commemorate events that had already taken place. Modern scholars sometimes point out that many of these topographical "baptisms" are attempts to make sense of pre-Israelite names whose origins were unknown and not understood, but even if that is often the case, it does not matter. By giving places comprehensible names related to historical events, the Israelites were claiming the territory for themselves and making the promised land their own. The significance of this was both spiritual and literal—spiritual because it spoke of the purposes of God for his people and literal because the land was configured to bear witness to those purposes. Once this was understood, it was quite easy to pass from Jewish understandings to Christian ones, since the spiritual meaning applied equally to both, if perhaps in a somewhat different way.

Jerome got most of his information and ideas from Origen, as he himself admitted. Nor did he see anything wrong with that. He writes, "[My critics say] that I compile from the books of Origen, and that it is not becoming for the writings of ancients to be plagiarized, which they think is a vehement curse. I regard this as very great praise. For I wish to imitate one who, I do not doubt, pleases you. . . . If it is a crime to translate the things well spoken by the Greeks, let them accuse Ennius, Virgil, Plautus, Caecilius, Terence and Cicero . . . who translated not only verses but many chapters and very long books and whole narratives."[19] What Jerome was doing had been done by Latin writers for centuries, and the key word is "translate." None of his readers would bother (or even be able) to read his sources in the original, so why not make them available to an eager public in a language they could understand?

Moreover, Jerome told his readers that he did not copy his sources exactly but edited them as he went along. When explaining his dependence on Didymus the Blind—and through him, Origen—when writing his commentary on Zechariah, he says, "I am saying these things so you will know the forerunners I have had in the field of this prophet. . . . I have not followed them in everything, [so] that I might be a judge rather than [just] a translator of their work and might say what I think in each case, and what I have received with much labor from one or another of my Jewish teachers."[20] Nor was this mere rhetoric. In his preface to Malachi,

Jerome writes, "Origen wrote three volumes on this book, but he did not touch the history [i.e., the literal sense] at all, and as is his custom he got completely involved in the allegorical interpretation. . . . We do not accept this interpretation at all. Otherwise we would be compelled to accept the fall of souls from heaven."[21]

The Ongoing Relevance of the Old Testament

Unlike Theodore of Mopsuestia, whom he often resembles in the way he treats the literal sense of the text, Jerome did not hesitate to apply Old Testament history to Christian circumstances without recourse to allegory. For example, when commenting on the corrupt offerings being made by the priests in the time of Malachi, Jerome says:

> The rule of the Scriptures is that when a very clear prophecy about the future is composed, one should not detract from what is written by means of uncertain allegories. Therefore, properly speaking, the word of the Lord is now being made to the priests of the Jews, who are offering in sacrifice the blind, the lame and the sick. This is so that they may know that spiritual victims will come in succession to the fleshly victims. And it is not the blood of bulls and goats that must be offered to the Lord, but "incense," that is, the prayers of the saints, and not in one province of the world, Judaea, nor in one city of Judaea, Jerusalem, but in every place the oblation is offered, not an unclean one, as from the people of Israel, but a clean one, as in the ceremonies of the Christians.[22]

Interestingly, Jerome was aware that his argument could be used by people who thought that Christian priests were just as corrupt as the ancient Jewish ones had been and that the words of Malachi could be transferred to refer to them as well. But if that were the case, said Jerome, then references to the sacrificial victims would also have to be transferred from the church to another religion. Little did he know that a few centuries later, that is precisely what some Muslims would argue in trying to justify the transfer of God's favor from the Christians to themselves![23]

Something similar can be found in Jerome's comments on Hosea 7:5–7. He recounted the sorry history of the kingdom of Israel as told in 2 Kings and then applied its lessons to the state of the church in his own time. As he puts it:

> All the kings of Israel fell and walked in the ways of Jeroboam son of Nebat, who made Israel sin, and no one was found who deserted idols and turned back to God. . . . Now let us pass over to the spiritual understanding [of this history]. It is an unhappy people that is seduced by the devil, their king, and by his princes, or who . . . have undertaken alien solemnities, leaving the church and who, trampling the truth of the faith, cry out and say: "This is the day of our king"—of [the heretics] Valentinus, Marcion, Arius and Eunomius.[24]

Jerome was acutely aware of the differences between the Hebrew text he was commenting on and the Septuagint version approved by the church, but he did his best to accommodate them both, believing that the underlying message was the same, despite the apparent differences. For example, Habakkuk 2:11 reads in the Hebrew: "For the stone shall cry out of the wall, and the timber that is between the joints of the building shall answer." The Septuagint however, says: "The stone shall cry out of the wall, and the beetle shall speak these things out of the timber."[25] On the other hand, as Jerome carefully notes, other Greek translations supported the Hebrew reading, particularly the one done by Symmachus, which he quoted at length.

So how can these different readings be reconciled? Jerome begins by establishing the historical context: "The words are being addressed to the man who is heaping up evils and a multitude of riches to himself. He does not understand that this is the cause of the ruin of his house. . . . This is what the prophet's words are signifying according to history: the stones of the walls and the burnt-up timber, since they have been demolished by you, shall resound your cruelty."[26] But rotting timber is an ideal home for beetles, who in Jerome's view stand for false teachers in the church. What he concludes therefore is this: "We can understand the 'stones' as the insensitive hearts of the believers in the doctrines of the heretics, and the 'beetle from the timber' as all perverse teachers who take up the preaching of the cross for the sake of base gain . . . to teach with a viper's mouth the covetousness and pride of their teacher the devil."[27] Jerome then rounds it all off by going back to the timber itself, saying that the teaching of the heretics speaks out of timber, for they are unable to convince in any other way but to prefer the glory of their timber to its perversity.[28] Both versions are thus merged together to proclaim a common message, the real difference not being between the Hebrew and the Greek but between the old and the new dispensations of the covenant.

It is obvious from the above that Jerome had a brilliant and fertile mind that could juggle many different sources and perspectives in ways that led to a common outcome. Careful readers might quibble with some of his arguments, but in the end they would probably agree with most of his conclusions and learn what to believe and what to avoid. A great interpreter of the Scriptures cannot expect more than that.

Back to the Sources

Jerome set the standard for all serious biblical interpretation because of his insistence that the study of the Bible be based on the original Hebrew and Greek texts. Translations are possible and need to not be misleading, but they are not the final word.

Jerome also reminds us that the literal sense is important both in historical and in spiritual terms. Learning the facts about the past matters because our faith is grounded in real events that have shaped our lives, but spiritual awareness is needed if we are to understand their meaning correctly. This does not mean that we have to allegorize or fantasize about what the Bible says, but we have to see its teaching in the light of eternal truths, which are easily forgotten in our secular age.

Jerome teaches us that every word of the Bible must be mastered and understood. Even if we can speak Hebrew or Greek, we are still separated from the context in which the texts were written and have to recognize that words have changed meaning over time. Because this is a subtle and gradual process, Hebrew and Greek speakers may actually be more easily misled than complete foreigners! Learning to think in a different language and culture is never easy, but Jerome shows us that it can and must be done.

The life of Jerome demonstrates how easily we can be led astray by our own prejudices if we are not careful. He was a product of his time, with all its advantages and limitations, and so are we. Reading him reminds us of what is possible but also what we need to be wary of. By being the genius that he was, he has given us a benchmark to measure our smaller minds against and a reminder to be humble in the presence of the giants who have gone before us.

● REFLECTION QUESTIONS ●

1. Jerome was a difficult person with an eccentric lifestyle. How important should things like that be when we try to estimate the value of someone's contribution to biblical studies? How tolerant should we be of unlikable character traits or behavior in teachers and preachers today?

2. Was Jerome justified in translating the same Hebrew and Greek words differently according to what he believed they meant in context, or should he have stuck to one word for each Hebrew and Greek term, leaving the reader to decide what it might mean in particular cases? How free can a translator be in trying to express meaning in another language?

● FURTHER READING ●

Translated Texts of Jerome

Archer, Gleason L., Jr., trans. *Jerome's Commentary on Daniel*. By Jerome. Baker, 1977.

Cain, Andrew, trans. *St. Jerome: Commentary on Galatians*. By Jerome. Catholic University of America Press, 2010.

Goodrich, Richard J., and David J. Miller, trans. *St. Jerome: Commentary on Ecclesiastes*. By Jerome. Newman Press, 2012.

Graves, Michael, trans. *Commentary on Jeremiah*. By Jerome. Edited by Christopher A. Hall. InterVarsity Press, 2011.

Heine, Ronald E., trans. *The Commentaries of Origen and Jerome on St. Paul's Epistle to the Ephesians*. By Jerome. Oxford University Press, 2001.

Scheck, Thomas P., trans. *St. Jerome: Commentary on Ezekiel*. By Jerome. Newman Press, 2017.

Scheck, Thomas P., trans. *St. Jerome's Commentaries on Galatians, Titus, and Philemon*. By Jerome. University of Notre Dame Press, 2010.

Scheck, Thomas P., trans. *St. Jerome: Commentary on Isaiah; Origen: Homilies 1–9 on Isaiah*. By Jerome. Paulist Press, 2015.

Scheck, Thomas P., trans. *St. Jerome: Commentary on Matthew*. By Jerome. Catholic University of America Press, 2008.

Scheck, Thomas P., trans. *St. Jerome: Commentary on the Twelve Prophets*. 2 vols. By Jerome. InterVarsity Press, 2016–2017.

White, Carolinne, trans. *The Correspondence (394–419) Between Jerome and Augustine of Hippo*. By Jerome. Edwin Mellen Press, 1990.

Studies

Brown, Dennis, and Vir Trilinguis. *A Study in the Biblical Exegesis of Saint Jerome*. Kok Pharos Publishing House, 1992.

Cain, Andrew. *Jerome's Commentaries on the Pauline Epistles and the Architecture of Exegetical Authority*. Oxford University Press, 2018.

Kelly, J. N. D. *Jerome: His Life, Writings, and Controversies*. Duckworth, 1975.

8

AUGUSTINE OF HIPPO

(AD 354–430)

Who He Was

Augustine was born on November 13, 354, in the North African town of Thagaste, which lay just west of what is now the border of Algeria and Tunisia. His ethnic origin is disputed, but whether he was African (Berber) or not, his culture and upbringing were indisputably Roman. His father, Patricius, was a pagan who converted to Christianity later in life, but his mother, Monica, was already a believer when Augustine was born. She wanted to have him baptized as a child after he had an illness that brought him near to death, but his father's paganism prevented that. He received the best education that Thagaste could offer and also studied at Carthage, where he became a teacher of rhetoric in 375. Before that, while he was still a student in Carthage, he embarked on a long-term relationship with a woman of inferior social standing. For that reason, they could not marry, but together they had a son named Adeodatus. In 384 he left North

Africa for Rome, and later in that year he went to Milan, where he continued to teach rhetoric. He was well-schooled in the Latin classics but had only schoolboy Greek and no Hebrew. His mother had given him a Christian education at home, but he had abandoned the church shortly before taking up his teaching post in Carthage.

Although Augustine refused to call himself a Christian at this stage of his life, he was tormented by a desire for wisdom and spiritual security. This led him to read Cicero's *Hortensius*, which initiated him into Greek philosophy, and for many years he was attached to the sect of the Manichaeans, who preached a rationalistic faith and claimed to have solved the problem of evil by saying that it was possible to turn away from it by rational decision. He never became a Manichaean himself and was unhappy with what he perceived to be an inadequate analysis of the human condition, but it was several years before he broke with them completely.

By then he was making a new life for himself in Italy, where he came under the sway of the preaching of Ambrose, the famous bishop of Milan. His spiritual anxieties returned, but as he listened to Ambrose, his resistance to Christianity began to crumble. Finally, he reached a point of spiritual crisis, when he read in Romans 13:12: "The night is far gone; the day is at hand. So then let us cast off the works of darkness and put on the armor of light." The message struck him like a thunderbolt, and he surrendered his life to Christ.

The newly converted Augustine struggled with his sexual desires, but in the end he gave up his concubine; refused to marry, despite his mother's hopes; and embarked on a life of consecrated celibacy. He became a catechumen (baptismal candidate) and followed a course of instruction before being baptized with his friend Alypius and his son Adeodatus on April 24, 387. The three men then decided to return to North Africa, where Augustine intended to create a monastic community. The death of his mother, who had followed him to Italy, delayed things somewhat, but in 388 he went back to Thagaste. In 391 he paid a visit to Hippo (now Annaba in Algeria), where he hoped to establish his community, but before that could happen, the church there insisted he be ordained a priest. After that he was able to pursue his dream, and he became a regular preacher and teacher in the city.

In 395 Augustine was consecrated as assistant to the elderly bishop of the city, and when that man died in 397, Augustine became bishop in his stead. For the rest of his life he remained in Hippo, preaching several times a week, organizing social welfare, settling legal disputes, and attending the many synods that the North African church held, mainly in Carthage. During this time he never stopped writing, and his surviving output is greater than that of any other church father. He died on August 28, 430, when the Vandals were besieging the city. Shortly afterward, the Vandals conquered the whole province, and Roman rule came to an end. Augustine's executor and biographer Possidius managed to save his library, so most of what he wrote has survived to the present time.

Augustine's Career

We know as much about Augustine as we do partly because of Possidius's efforts as a biographer, but mostly because of Augustine's *Confessions*, a book in which he described his early life and conversion. The *Confessions* are unique in that they are framed as a prayer to God for grace and forgiveness, and it is this deeply personal touch that has made them a spiritual classic that nobody since has been able to imitate. It is obviously difficult to untangle the facts of Augustine's life from his perception of them, but that scarcely matters. What is certain is that we meet Augustine the man as he saw himself, and we also meet God as Augustine saw him. The story has the ring of truth about it and leaves its mark on all who have read it, whether they are believers or not.

Augustine was a great man in every sense of the word, and his personality shines clearly in his writings. In the course of his career, he covered a wide range of subjects, discoursing authoritatively on the Trinity, the church, salvation, and the Scriptures, along with much else. There is hardly anything he did not touch on at some point, and his works have been an encyclopedic source of inspiration for centuries.

It is not too much to say that Western Christianity as we know it is the creation of Augustine, not in its fundamentals, which predated his time and are shared with all Christians, but in its intellectual shape and priorities. Theological themes like grace and predestination would not have occupied the attention of Western theologians to the degree that they have were it not for him. Proof of this can be seen in the Eastern churches, where his influence was not felt to anything like the same extent—his works were not translated into Greek until the late thirteenth century—and where theological discourse has taken a very different turn. In the West, however, his thought has often been the main impulse for religious revival, and the great theologians of later times, such as Anselm of Canterbury (1033–1109), Thomas Aquinas (1225–1274), Martin Luther (1483–1546), and John Calvin (1509–1564) have all been Augustinian to a greater or lesser degree.

Pride of place among Augustine's writings belongs to his sermons, of which about five hundred still survive, representing perhaps a tenth of the total. They are mostly based on Scripture and are important for how they reflect the state of the church in his time, the nature of his pastoral ministry, and the thought patterns that went into the making of his great theological works. Also of importance here are his letters—about three hundred have been identified—which shed light on the controversies he was involved in and the people he had to deal with. Like the sermons, they extend over the whole of his active career and show how he developed and expanded his thinking over time.

The Donatist Schism

It is impossible in a short introduction to look at everything he wrote, but Augustine is unique in that some of his more important works are still in print today and can easily be purchased in a number of different translations. Others are less widely read, but their impact on church history has been considerable, and we cannot understand his life without considering them as well.

For example, there is a whole series of books and treatises directed against the Donatists, a schismatic sect in North Africa that broke away from the mainline church following the legalization of Christianity in 313. One of the leaders of the schism was Donatus, and although he was not its original instigator, it is named after him. Donatism was the belief that the church had been compromised by legalization. To Donatists, it was the calling of Christians to suffer persecution for their faith, a belief that rested on New Testament passages like Matthew 5:11–12. There is undoubtedly an element of truth in this, as the North African theologian Tertullian (ca. 200) remarked when he claimed that "the blood of martyrs is the seed of the church."[1] A church that is not persecuted must ask itself why, and if the answer is that it is because Christians have conformed to the standards of this world, then a reaction is clearly necessary.

The Donatists, however, took things too far. As zealots often do, they went looking for trouble and were not slow to condemn other Christians they suspected of compromising their faith. In their desire for purity, they became fanatics—and hypocrites, too, because nobody can live a perfect life. In combating them, Augustine had to work out what salvation means: It is not perfection in this life, but the promise of heavenly reward to those who put their trust in Christ. As believers we do not become better people; instead, we realize that even if we do everything we are commanded to do, we are still "unworthy servants," in constant need of the grace of God and his forgiveness (Luke 17:10).

Donatism was a schism, not a heresy, which means it split the church but did not teach any false doctrines, as these were defined by the great church councils of Nicaea and Constantinople. It was therefore possible for Augustine to oppose the Donatists because of their limited understanding while at the same time acknowledging that they might have valuable things to say on other subjects. At least one Donatist, a man called Tyconius, was a gifted Bible teacher, and Augustine did not hesitate to adopt his rules for biblical interpretation, giving full credit to him in the process. The schism was also confined to North Africa, which allowed Augustine to portray it as a local aberration that was not of fundamental importance for the church as a whole. He did what he could to end the schism, but despite some success, he could not stamp it out altogether. Donatism survived in North Africa as long as Christianity did, and it was only after the Muslim conquest in 698 that it finally died out.

The Pelagian Heresy

The other major problem that Augustine had to confront was Pelagianism, named after a British teacher called Pelagius who had gone to Rome and made his career there sometime around 400.[2] Pelagius taught, or was believed to teach, that human beings can cooperate in our salvation because we are not totally ruined (or "depraved," to use the somewhat misleading theological term) by our fall into sin. To Augustine, this was like trying to build a house on sand, because salvation in Christ could not possibly be grounded in human effort of any kind. Augustine came across this heresy—and it was a heresy (false teaching), not merely a schism—in 411 when he attended a synod at Carthage that was summoned in order to resolve the Donatist controversy. Pelagius had turned up there following the sack of Rome by the Goths in the previous year, and he was winning converts. Augustine turned on him and eventually had him driven out of North Africa, but for the rest of his life he did battle with the Pelagians.

Augustine believed that Pelagianism was more dangerous than Donatism because it flattered the human ego, allowing it to think that it could play a role in making us more like God. He was right to think that, because every time the gospel has been preached in power, the specter of human cooperation with God has reappeared. In the seventeenth century, it came in the form of Arminianism, and today it is often associated with Celtic or New Age spirituality. It has all the appearance of godliness but denies its power (2 Tim. 3:5). Circumstances change over time, but the underlying temptation to dilute the gospel message remains the same, and the danger is as insidious now as it was in Augustine's day.

The basic challenge of Pelagianism is that it opposes the totally fallen nature of human beings, who can do nothing to save themselves. This unhappy situation has come about because our first parents obeyed Satan rather than God and were trapped in a cycle of evil that cannot now be broken without divine intervention. It is tempting to think that children are born innocent and that they become evil by imitation, but a moment's thought will show that this cannot be right. After all, if an infant who dies before reaching the age of discernment is guaranteed to go to heaven, why should anyone grow up and lose their salvation?

Yet the message of Scripture is that we must not remain like babies but come to the full maturity of the adult human being. Nobody is exempt from this, because "all have sinned and fall short of the glory of God" (Rom. 3:23). Augustine advocated the baptism of infants, not so much because he thought that baptism would save them, but because water baptism is a sign reminding us that all human beings need to die to themselves and be born again in Christ. There are no exceptions, and dying young is not an alternative to profession of faith in Christ as a way of getting into heaven.

The Kingdoms of This World and the City of God

That Pelagianism should come to Augustine's notice at the same time that news of the fall of Rome reached him may have been a coincidence, but it was no accident, because in a sense the two things went together. Augustine watched as the Roman Empire was falling apart, a disaster that traumatized the entire ancient world. Some pagans blamed this on the Christians, claiming that if the Romans had stuck with their ancestral gods, they would have saved the city from destruction. Augustine sensed that this was wrong, but in order to make his point, he had to embark on a complete overhaul of human history as it had been understood by the Romans up to that time.

As he saw it, the history of the world is a battle between good and evil, good being represented by the divine revelation originally given to Israel and fulfilled in Christ, and evil by the powers of this world that rise up in rebellion against the purposes of God. Seen in this light, Rome was but the latest in a series of empires that would rise and fall over time. Such empires appear to be all-powerful and offer their subjects a kind of peace and salvation, but this is an illusion, and sooner or later they come crashing down. What had happened to Assyria, Babylonia, and Persia in the past was now happening to Rome and would happen again when other states would arise to claim an authority that belongs to God alone.

On the other side stands the "city of God," which is represented in the Bible as Jerusalem or Zion but in reality includes all those who believe in Christ.[3] The city of God can be exiled, it can be physically destroyed, it can be subjected to foreign rulers—but it will never disappear, because its ruler is the sovereign Lord of heaven and earth. To get this point across, Augustine had to develop theological themes that were latent in the Bible but had not figured very prominently in most Christian teaching after the close of the New Testament era. The most characteristic doctrine here was what we call predestination but what is more properly referred to as the sovereignty of God. This means that God is both the Creator and the Ruler of the universe that he has made. Human beings have the capacity to rebel against him, just as Satan did, but no rebellion can ever succeed. In the end, as Paul put it, "every knee should bow, in heaven and on earth and under the earth, and every tongue confess that Jesus Christ is Lord, to the glory of God the Father" (Phil. 2:10–11). This does not mean that everybody will be saved in the end—those who accept the lordship of Christ will go to be with him in heaven, while those who reject it will be cast into the darkness of hell. But whether they are in heaven or hell, all created things will one day acknowledge God as their Lord and be subject to his power.

The practical consequence of this is that those who believe in Christ must think of themselves in a different way. The apostle Paul laid down the principle in Galatians 3:28: "There is neither Jew nor Greek, there is neither slave nor free, there is no male and female, for you are all one in Christ Jesus." To become a Christian is to be set free from the limitations of our human tribes and nations and to be united with one another in the universal people of God. For Augustine and his readers, that meant giving up the ancient Romans—pagan Roman religion was essentially an ancestor cult—and embracing Abraham, Isaac, and Jacob instead. The history of the Old Testament people of God and the inheritance of the new Israel in Christ are what matter now, and our whole way of thinking must change. People will no longer name their children Romulus or Remus, the legendary founders of their city, but choose names from the New Testament—Peter, Paul, John, Mary—in conscious self-identification with them as our ancestors in the faith. That this is still true today is the legacy of Augustine, who took seriously Paul's teaching about Gentiles being grafted into the tree of Israel and applied it to the practicalities of daily living.[4]

The Holy Trinity

If Augustine had never done anything else, his fame would have been secured by this, but he did not stop at this point. He went on to expound the revelation of God in Scripture and its relationship to humanity in general. The God of the Bible is a Trinity of three persons in one substance. Augustine did not invent that doctrine, but he developed its significance both for our salvation and for our relationship with God. Working from the principle that God is love, Augustine said that for love to be real, there must be a Lover, a Beloved, and a bond of Love that unites them. The Lover is the Father, the Beloved is the Son, and the Love that binds them is the Holy Spirit. All three must be equal and active in God's self-revelation, because all three are manifestations of the one Lord. The analogy may not be perfect—analogies never are—but this way of thinking about God has dominated Western civilization ever since, and we cannot understand it if we do not recognize this.

Tied to this is the doctrine that human beings are created in the image and likeness of God.[5] Augustine understood this psychologically, seeing the human mind in trinitarian terms. All human minds are a combination of memory, intellect, and will, and they cannot function properly unless all three elements are fully engaged. They can be distinguished from one another and even re-created to some extent—a computer has a memory and a kind of intellect, but it has no will, because it is not created in the image of God the Holy Trinity! Augustine did not know it, but in saying this he not only defined the relationship between humanity and God but foreshadowed the later scientific discipline of psychology, which could never have come into being without an analysis of this kind. Furthermore, this resemblance establishes the fact that God and humanity stand together over the rest of creation. We can communicate with each other and share a common life together in a way that is not possible with animals, let alone with plants or inorganic matter.

Adam, representing humanity, is given dominion over the creatures, even though he is a creature himself, and it is his duty to order the world in a way that reflects the sovereignty of the God to whom he is ultimately responsible. The linchpin of all this is Jesus Christ, the Son of God who became human in order to save us from our sins and make us coheirs with him of eternal life. Here indeed was a worldview capable of overthrowing paganism, which it proceeded to do. Our world would not have been the same without it.

How Augustine Read the Bible

Augustine was not a biblical scholar in the same sense that Jerome was, nor was he a preacher and teacher of the Bible like John Chrysostom and Theodore of Mopsuestia, his Eastern contemporaries. Given the enormous range of his work, his expositions of Scripture are relatively few and far between. Many of them are collections of questions put to him by various people about particular topics in certain biblical books (notably Genesis through Judges, the Gospels, and Romans), and some are notes of his put together by others (Job and James). One of his favorite biblical passages was the creation narrative in Genesis 1–3, which he wrote on no fewer than four times. One of his treatises was meant to be a literal exposition of the text, but in fact it often resorts to allegory; another is an unfinished tract he wrote at the beginning of his career and soon abandoned; and a third is attached to his *Confessions*. In the New Testament, he wrote on the Sermon on the Mount and also produced a harmony of the Gospels that would inspire later generations to look for a way of combining them into a single narrative. He also started to write a commentary on Romans but never finished it.

Beyond that, Augustine managed to put together a complete set of meditations on the Psalms, the only one of its kind to have survived from ancient times. It assumes that the Psalter is a revelation of Christ—sometimes he is speaking, and sometimes others are speaking about him, but he is always at the center of the meditations. Augustine also wrote a series of tracts on John's Gospel and on 1 John, in which the main theme is love (charity). These are profound meditations on the biblical texts in question, but they are devotional works and avoid the kind of critical questions normally found in commentaries. These works are interesting and important in their own right, but to understand how Augustine viewed the Bible as a whole, we must look elsewhere.

The Bible as Christian Doctrine

Fortunately, Augustine has left us one of the most important books of biblical interpretation ever written. This is his *De doctrina Christiana* (*On Christian Doctrine*), which is still in print today and is highly regarded in theological circles. To appreciate it, we must begin by understanding how Augustine viewed the world in general. For him, the basic division was between the material and the nonmaterial (or spiritual) dimensions of reality. Human beings live in material creation, which is the natural framework in which our minds operate, but creation points beyond itself to the realm of the Creator, which is more fundamental and therefore more important. As the apostle Paul put it, "The things that are seen are transient, but the things that are unseen are eternal" (2 Cor. 4:18). The relationship between the two can be expressed in two ways—one of them is objective and the other subjective, or experiential.

The objective relationship is between material signs (*signa*) and the nonmaterial things they signify (*significata* or *res significatae*). Every material object is a sign of something higher that the thoughtful person—and all Christian believers are called to be thoughtful people—would discern. This can be seen in Augustine's view of the sacraments of baptism and the Lord's Supper. He linked water baptism to spiritual regeneration, but this connection must not be misunderstood. To be baptized in water is not a guarantee of spiritual rebirth but only a sign pointing toward it. As he writes in one of his treatises on John's Gospel, "Why does John not say: 'You are clean because of the baptism with which you were washed,' but 'because of the word which I have spoken to you,' unless the reason is that even in the water it is the word which cleanses? Take away the word and what is the water but [plain] water? But when the word comes into association with the material element a sacrament comes into being, as though the word itself took visible form."[6] The "word" of course is the voice of the Holy Spirit, whose presence cannot be conjured up by a ritual act, no matter how indicative of his saving work that act may be.

The same is true of the Lord's Supper, where the elements of bread and wine are signs of the body and blood of Christ, not the body and blood themselves. That aberration would emerge in the Middle Ages in the guise of transubstantiation, which the Protestant Reformers of the sixteenth century rejected. In the words of Article 28 of the Church of England, "Transubstantiation . . . cannot be proved by holy Writ, but is repugnant to the plain words of Scripture, overthroweth the nature of a sacrament, and hath given occasion to many superstitions. The Body of Christ is given, taken and eaten, in the Supper, only after an heavenly and spiritual manner."[7] Augustine would have approved.

Given this mentality, we should not be surprised to hear him say that the Bible itself is a sign that points to a higher reality beyond it. The Bible is given to us by God because there is no other way that he can communicate with us effectively, and it is a sure guide to the heavenly things of which it speaks. The Holy Spirit speaks to us in and through it, but he does so in order to take us into the presence of God, which is a spiritual experience distinct from the words on the printed page. The words are an infallible guide to that experience for those who pay attention to them, but they are not the experience themselves. To read the

Bible is therefore to discover in and through it that "peace of God, which surpasses all understanding" (Phil. 4:7).

It is here that the subjective or experiential aspect of our relationship with God comes into play. The Bible is a material means that we are meant to use (*uti*) so that we can enjoy (*frui*) what it's pointing us toward.[8] To put it a different way, it is the means to an end, not the end in itself. Once we understand that, the secrets of Scripture start to unfold. Manuscripts copied by hand almost always contain mistakes, most of them unintentional. Augustine teaches us how to recognize these and correct them. But there are also passages that are mysterious and not susceptible to easy interpretation. These passages are not corrupted or false but have been put there by God in order to test our spiritual maturity. Anyone who has done a crossword puzzle or run a race will understand this. Some puzzles and races are easy and are meant to encourage beginners. Others get progressively harder as the novice matures. The really skilled players have the hardest hurdles to overcome, and they are the ones who become the teachers of others who are less advanced on their spiritual journey. God does not want anyone to turn away from the Bible on the grounds that it is too easy and boring—he wants his followers to be excited by difficulties, just as the apostles wanted their congregations to advance from the "milk" of the Word of God to its "meat," from liquid baby food to solid adult food (1 Cor. 3:1–3 KJV).[9]

Inevitably, an analysis of the signs of the biblical text will lead to some form of spiritual interpretation, especially when the literal meaning is unacceptable or inapplicable for some reason. That has always been the case, of course, and Origen led the way in developing the "higher" senses of Scripture as a way of explaining these difficulties. Augustine followed suit, but in a different way. Instead of thinking in terms of body, soul, and spirit, as Origen had done, he preferred to speak about faith, hope, and love (charity) as the three stages of spiritual growth leading to maturity.[10] As Christians, we begin by reading the Bible in faith—everything in it points us somehow to God. We then go on to hope, because faith in what is and has been must always serve a purpose that, from our temporal point of view, is in the future—we are pilgrims on the way to our home in the heavenly Jerusalem. What that is and what we will be like when we get there are revealed by love, because God is love—the most basic and constantly recurring theme in Augustine's writings.

Often this progression is not too difficult, but sometimes it can be. Take Psalm 137 for example. That Psalm was written by a Jewish exile who was devastated by the fall of Jerusalem to the Babylonians and the terrible fate that was meted out on the chosen people of God. In response to that, he gave his emotions free rein: "Blessed shall he be who repays you with what you have done to us! Blessed shall he be who takes your little ones and dashes them against the rock!" (vv. 8–9). The original circumstances may be understandable, but the sentiment expressed here is hardly in agreement with the Word of God when taken literally. The psalmist may have faith that God will avenge their people, they may have hope that this revenge will not be long delayed, but can it be said that there is anything of love in words like these? Augustine knew that there was not, but he also knew that this verse has an important message for Christians. That message can only be unlocked by applying a spiritual sense to it. Babylon stands for the world in rebellion against God, and the sufferers are his chosen people—the church. Augustine explains it like this:

> When we were born, the confusion of this world found us, and while we were still children it choked us with the empty ideas of various errors. The child that is destined to become a citizen of Jerusalem, and who in God's predestination is already a citizen, is a prisoner [of this world] for a time. He can only learn to love what his parents whisper in his ears. They teach and train him in greed, theft, lying, the worship of idols and other superstitions. . . . In this way Babylon persecuted us when we were little, but

when we grew up God gave us knowledge of ourselves, so that
we should not follow the errors of our parents. . . . What are the
little ones of Babylon? Evil desires at their birth. . . . When lust is
born, before it takes hold of you, do not let it gain the strength of
evil habit. Dash it while it is still small. Dash it against the Rock,
and that Rock is Christ.[11]

Modern students of Scripture may not want to follow Augustine's nonliteral interpretation at this point, but it is hard to deny
that he found an ingenious way of making the verse relevant to
our spiritual lives, even when the text expresses sentiments that
on the surface are alien to our faith in Christ. From a scholarly
point of view he may have been wrong, but in pastoral terms he
taught his people an important lesson that would do far more to
bring them into the presence of God than a literal reenactment
of the psalmist's wishes would have done.

The Foundation of Western Christianity

Without Augustine's massive contribution to Christian thought,
Western Christianity (both Roman Catholic and Protestant) would
not be what it is today. Virtually every major topic that comes up
in discussion today has been shaped by Augustinian thinking,
and without him, our mental universe would look quite different.

Augustine had a coherent worldview built around the idea that
God is love and that we have been created in his image. These are
biblical concepts, of course, but Augustine tied them together and
gave us a particular way of looking at them that still influences
our culture today.

Augustine's teaching is vital because every time we human
beings start to think that we are not all that bad and that we can
somehow save ourselves, he comes to remind us that this is not so.
If anyone is saved, it is because of God's grace, freely given to those
who believe in Jesus Christ. There is no other way of salvation,

and in God's kingdom everybody he has chosen is treated equally. Human hierarchies have been overthrown by his spiritual power, and Augustine is a major witness to that.

Augustine shows us that faith is not simply belief in a set of truths but a life that must be lived in fellowship with God. The outward signs of Christian profession are no substitute for the enjoyment of the things that they signify, and Augustine pushes us to deeper and broader self-examination as we seek to draw closer to God.

Rewriting the history of the world, Augustine put Christ at the center. Today we calculate time either as before Christ (BC) or as "in the year of the Lord" (*anno Domini*, or AD). Augustine did not invent the Christian calendar, but he made it possible, and now people around the world follow it. Christ is recognized as the Lord of time because Augustine said he was and went to great lengths to demonstrate that.

We see in Augustine's life how God can take anyone and use them for his glory. Augustine led a godless life for many years, but God turned him around. He ministered in a provincial backwater with very few resources at his disposal. He had to struggle against schisms and heresies that threatened to destroy the church. But God took him from this unpromising background and turned him into one of the greatest witnesses to Christian faith who has ever lived. What God did for Augustine he can do for any of us if we die to ourselves and are born again by his Holy Spirit. No one is too bad or too humble to be used by God—that is perhaps the greatest lesson that Augustine has to teach us.

● **REFLECTION QUESTIONS** ●

1. How should we see the events of our lives from a spiritual perspective? How open should we be about past sins and failures? Was Augustine too hard on himself?

2. Is human history the account of an ongoing struggle between good and evil? Why does God allow his creatures
to rebel against him?

● FURTHER READING ●

Translated Texts of Augustine[12]

Bettenson, Henry, trans. *City of God.* By Augustine. Edited by David
Knowles. Penguin, 1972.

Chadwick, Henry, trans. *Confessions.* By Augustine. Oxford University
Press, 1991.

Studies

Arnold, Duane W. H., and Pamela Bright, eds. *De doctrina Christiana: A
Classic of Western Culture.* University of Notre Dame Press, 1995.

Bray, Gerald L. *Augustine on the Christian Life: Transformed by the Power of
God.* Crossway, 2015.

Demacopoulos, George E., and Aristotle Papanikolaou, eds. *Orthodox
Readings of Augustine.* St. Vladimir's Seminary Press, 2008.

Evans, Gillian R. *Augustine on Evil.* Cambridge University Press, 1982.

Fitzgerald, Allan D., ed. *Augustine Through the Ages: An Encyclopedia.* Eerdmans, 1999.

Frend, W. H. C. *The Donatist Church: A Movement of Protest in Roman
North Africa.* Clarendon Press, 1952.

Meconi, David V., and Eleonore Stump. *The Cambridge Companion to
Augustine.* 2nd ed. Cambridge University Press, 2014.

Patte, Daniel, and Eugene TeSelle. *Engaging Augustine on Romans: Self,
Context, and Theology in Interpretation.* Trinity Press International, 2002.

Rigby, Paul. *Original Sin in Augustine's Confessions.* University of Ottawa
Press, 1987.

Rist, John M. *Augustine: Ancient Thought Baptized.* Cambridge University
Press, 1994.

Sullivan, John E. *The Image of God: The Doctrine of St. Augustine and Its
Influence.* The Priory Press, 1963.

CYRIL OF ALEXANDRIA

(ca. AD 376–444)

Who He Was

Cyril was born to a prominent Christian family in Alexandria sometime around 376, but the details of his early life are obscure. As a young man, he may have spent some time with the desert monks outside the city, but this is uncertain, and Cyril himself never mentioned it. He first comes to our attention in 403, when he went to Constantinople with his uncle Theophilus, who was Alexandria's bishop (patriarch), and there he witnessed the deposition of John Chrysostom. Theophilus had a grudge against John, perhaps because John came from Antioch, Alexandria's rival city in the East, and Cyril seems to have inherited that. He succeeded his uncle as patriarch in 412, despite some opposition from the government, and carried on Theophilus's policies, at least for a time. Chrysostom was eventually rehabilitated in the eyes of the Alexandrian church, but Theophilus's policy of persecuting Jews, pagans, and heretics continued. In 415 the pagan philosopher

Hypatia was torn to pieces by an angry mob in the city, and the church historian Socrates hinted that Cyril was implicated in that murder, although there is no evidence to suggest that he was.[1] But the fact that such an accusation was plausible tells us much about Cyril's somewhat unsavory reputation, which made him a controversial figure in the church politics of his time.

For many years Cyril governed his diocese fairly strictly and did what he could to rid it of any lingering Arianism. He also wrote a number of commentaries on different biblical books in which he upheld the trinitarian orthodoxy of the Councils of Nicaea and Constantinople. He only came to wider prominence around 428, when Nestorius of Antioch became patriarch of Constantinople. Alexandria had long regarded both Antioch and Constantinople as rivals, but in this case, the election of Nestorius was unsettling for theological as well as political reasons. Nestorius wasted no time in attacking heretics who had taken refuge in the capital, and prominent among them were the Apollinarians, followers of Apollinaris, who had been condemned at the First Council of Constantinople because he denied the full humanity of Christ. His heresy had also been condemned by the Alexandrian church, but the fact that Apollinaris saw himself as the theological heir of the great Athanasius, who had been patriarch of that city for nearly half a century (328–373) cast a shadow over it. Cyril suspected that Nestorius thought that all Alexandrians were tainted with Apollinarianism. If that were true, then persecuting people from Alexandria could be justified, and Cyril feared that his church would suffer as a result.

Nestorianism

But that was not all. Nestorius was teaching that the incarnate Christ had two distinct identities, one divine and the other human. To understand this properly, we must realize that for both Cyril and Nestorius, the words "God" and "man" weren't thought of in personal terms, as they are today, but meant what we would now call "divinity" and "humanity." Therefore to say that Jesus was "fully God and fully man" was to say that he was fully divine and fully human. But "divinity" and "humanity" are generic terms that do not exist in the abstract. In reality, they could only be perceived if they took on a specific form or identity, which was their particular *hypostasis*. For Nestorius, that meant that each of them had to have their own *hypostasis*, giving them a distinct identity that in theory would allow them to exist independently of the other. In practice, however, these two *hypostases* were conjoined in Mary's womb and came into the world as a single phenomenon, which Nestorius called their "person" (*prosōpon*). When we see Jesus, what we see is this "person" in whom we detect the underlying conjunction of divinity and humanity.

This all may sound very theoretical, but Nestorius's teaching becomes clearer when we ask, as Cyril did, whether the Virgin Mary could properly be called *Theotokos* ("God-bearer") or not. Nestorius admitted that she could be because the *hypostasis* of the Son of God was present in her womb, but to his mind this was a lopsided view of the incarnation. To do justice to that, Mary should also be called *anthrōpotokos* ("human-bearer"), because the embryo in her womb was also a human being. Of course, such dual terminology is cumbersome and to some extent faintly ridiculous, since every person who gets pregnant is a "human-bearer" and there is nothing particularly miraculous about that. What Nestorius preferred therefore was a third term, *Christotokos* ("Christ-bearer"), which described the "person" (*prosōpon*) formed by the conjunction between God and man in Mary's womb.

Prosōpon was not a new term, but it had rarely been used in theology before. It came from the theater, where it meant "mask." The actors would wear different masks in order to indicate the characters they were playing, and audiences would recognize who they were supposed to be. Over time, the word developed the meaning of "face" and was used for real faces as well as for masks.

When the apostle Paul told the Corinthians that "now we see in a mirror dimly, but then face to face," *prosōpon* is the word he used for "face" (1 Cor. 13:12). If we look at the context, though, we see that Paul turned the word's original meaning on its head, because to see God "face to face" was to see him *unmasked* (or "unveiled," as he would have put it). For Nestorius, to see Christ "face to face" was not to see God or man as such, but to see the conjunction of the two, which in effect was to see how the underlying realities made their appearance in public. He did not think of this as a "mask," but in effect it was, because the appearance of a conjunction could always give way to its component parts, which is what supposedly happened on the cross, when divinity abandoned humanity, leaving the latter to cry out, "My God, my God, why have you forsaken me?" (Matt. 27:46).

To Cyril, this was anathema. In his view, there could only be one *hypostasis* in the incarnate Christ. Since the Son of God exists in eternity and it was him who became human, that one *hypostasis* had to be divine. It followed that the humanity that the Son acquired in Mary's womb did not have a *hypostasis* of its own and therefore could not have existed independently of the Son of God. But how could "humanity" exist without a distinct identity of its own? One possibility was that it or parts of it could have been absorbed into the Son's divinity, which is basically what Apollinaris taught. But a divinized humanity would not have been a complete man. Without a human soul, the incarnate Christ could not have become sin for us and could not have suffered and died for us on the cross. Cyril recognized the problem and tried to solve it by saying that Christ's humanity was complete and retained its characteristics after the incarnation, but that it was permanently united by and in the Son's divine *hypostasis*, who could operate in his divinity or in both his divinity and his humanity as he chose. What he could not do was function as a man apart from his divinity, because apart from that he did not exist. Jesus was not a *prosōpon* in the Nestorian sense, but a divine *hypostasis*, and those who met him met the Son of God face-to-face.

It was at this point that the lack of a well-defined theological vocabulary caused problems for Cyril. To describe the divinity and humanity of Christ before the incarnation, he used the term *physis* ("nature"). Along with everybody else, he agreed that initially there were two of these, each with its own integrity, but that only the divine *physis* had a *hypostasis*—the Son of God. The human *physis* remained in Mary and was only given to the Son when she conceived Jesus. That conception was the work of the Holy Spirit, but the baby in her womb was God, making the title *Theotokos* not only appropriate, but essential. To reinforce this point, Cyril called Mary "Mother of God" (*Mētēr tou Theou*), an ambiguous term that could be understood to mean that she was the mother of Christ's divinity, which is not what *Theotokos* implied.[2] To someone like Nestorius, however, this could easily be mistaken for Apollinarianism, especially as Cyril saw no need to use words like *anthrōpotokos* or *Christotokos* when describing Mary.

But Cyril also said that the baby in Mary's womb was a single *physis*, which led to further confusion and misunderstanding. Was this single *physis* a combination of the two preincarnation *physeis* that had somehow merged into one, or was it something altogether new—a single "nature" formed out of two original "natures" in an indissoluble union? Cyril taught the second of these two options, but as a result, *physis* had to bear two different meanings. The "one nature" after the incarnation was the nature of the *hypostasis*, which was divine, while the "two natures" perceived before the incarnation remained distinct. The divine *physis* had real existence in the eternal Son of God and was shared with the Father and the Holy Spirit in their common "being" (*ousia*), whereas the human *physis*, though potentially present in Mary, remained essentially theoretical until she conceived. In other words, Cyril ended up saying that the incarnate Christ was both one nature and two, depending on how you look at it. For him, of course, it was the one *hypostasis* that really mattered, and he tended to downplay any postincarnation duality of natures, something that once again suggested to his opponents that he was a secret Apollinarian.

Cyril Versus Nestorius

How should we evaluate these different positions? Neither Cyril nor Nestorius had the perfect formula for describing the incarnate Christ, but we must admit that Cyril's understanding was superior. This was because he saw that the incarnation had to have an agent to initiate it. How could divinity and humanity have met and agreed to form a conjunction? Did the Son of God approach the baby Jesus of Nazareth and strike some kind of deal with him? That would have been absurd. The initiative had to come from the Son of God, who acquired a human nature from Mary that would not otherwise have existed. Cyril appealed his case against Nestorius to Rome, where Pope Celestine I (422–432) agreed with him. Celestine sent his decision back to Cyril and asked him to forward it to Nestorius in Constantinople.

It was an extraordinary request, and Cyril took advantage of the situation to add twelve anathemas of his own to Celestine's letter without the pope's knowledge. In these anathemas, also known as the twelve chapters, Cyril outlined the most bluntly anti-Nestorian position he could think of. Something of their tone can be gathered from the first and last of them: "If anyone does not confess that Emmanuel is truly God, and hence that the holy virgin is the Mother of God (for she gave birth in the flesh to the Word of God made flesh), let him be anathema. . . . If anyone does not confess that the Word of God suffered in the flesh, was crucified in the flesh, and tasted death in the flesh, becoming the first-born from the dead, although as God he is life and life-giving, let him be anathema."[3]

Cyril would spend much of the rest of his life backtracking from his bluntness and trying to explain to people what he really meant by statements like these. For example, he had to explain that Mary was not the "Mother of God" in the sense of being the source of divinity. Nor could the Word of God suffer and die in his divine nature, but only in the human nature that he had to assume for that purpose, though if divine and human were indissolubly united in a single nature, it is hard to see how such a distinction could be maintained. These explanations were meant to clarify Cyril's position, but it is not hard to see why the Nestorians were offended by his unsubtle approach.

The upshot was that in 431 the emperor Theodosius II (408–445) summoned a church council to meet at Ephesus, where Nestorius was condemned and deposed. The council was a shambles, with the church of Alexandria, supported by Rome, lining up against Antioch (the home of Nestorius), and the atmosphere was so poisoned by then that nothing was really resolved, even though Nestorius was forced out of Constantinople. After two years of negotiations forced on the rival groups by Theodosius II, Cyril conceded that it was possible to speak of two "natures" in Christ after the incarnation, even though he did not like to do so, and the Antiochenes went along with the condemnation of Nestorius, though many of them did not like that either.

Looking at this from the vantage point of centuries of historical distance, it is perhaps best to say that Cyril and Nestorius did not understand each other because they were addressing the question of Christ's identity from opposite perspectives. Nestorius began with Jesus of Nazareth, the human revealed to us in the Gospels, and asked what he was made of. It was an inductive approach, taking such things as the miracles of Jesus as signs of his divinity and then asking how that could be manifested in his self-evident humanity.

Cyril, on the other hand, started with the Trinity—three *hypostases* in the one God, one of which, the Son, became human. It was the perspective stated in the prologue to John's Gospel and developed both there and in other New Testament writings like the Epistle to the Hebrews. In contrast to Nestorius, Cyril's approach was deductive, explaining the incarnation of Christ as the conscious act of the divine Son, which, in theological terms, it had to be. Both men were trying to address the same fundamental questions, but Cyril's method was truer to the biblical revelation than Nestorius's was, and it was for that reason that his approach—although somewhat modified, to be sure—triumphed in the end.

Cyril of Alexandria is now celebrated by everyone except the dwindling minority of Nestorians as a hero of the faith and leading expounder of orthodox doctrine, but this common ground is not as solid as it might appear. Extremist followers of Cyril were not happy with his willingness to compromise on the "two natures" question, and they rejected it after his death. These so-called Monophysites ("one naturists") are now sometimes known as Copts (from a corruption of the word "Egypt") and are still the dominant form of indigenous Christianity in Egypt, Ethiopia, South India, and Armenia (in a slightly different form). Relations between them and the rest of the Christian world are nowadays quite good, and it is sometimes acknowledged that the differences between them are not as fundamental as they once appeared to be. It remains to be seen whether the Monophysites will ever accept, as Cyril did, that it is possible to speak of two natures in Christ after the incarnation, but it is safe to say that unless they do, the age-old separation seems destined to continue.

How Cyril Read the Bible

Cyril of Alexandria was a prolific writer who spent the early part of his episcopal career writing biblical commentaries in defense of the Nicene doctrine of the Trinity against the heresies of Arianism and Sabellianism, both of which had been condemned at Nicaea in 325 and again at Constantinople in 381.[4] Before the outbreak of the Nestorian controversy, he had already written on various questions arising from the Pentateuch, as well as commentaries on Isaiah, the Minor Prophets, and the Psalter, although all trace of that last one has been lost. In the New Testament, he wrote on Romans, 1 and 2 Corinthians, and Hebrews, as well as on the Gospels of Matthew, Luke, and John. The last of these survives almost intact and is universally recognized as a major contribution to orthodox trinitarian theology.

None of these commentaries mention Nestorius because they were written before his Christology had come to Cyril's attention. In his later career, Cyril did not revise them or write others addressing the Nestorian conflict in particular, but he did analyze the sources of Nestorius's beliefs. He knew that Nestorius was not much of a biblical theologian and suspected that he had gotten his ideas from Theodore of Mopsuestia, who he probably studied under in Antioch. He therefore trained his guns on Theodore (and on Theodore's teacher, Diodore of Tarsus, who he regarded as the true author of Nestorianism). It was his polemical writings against Theodore that were so influential in the condemnation of the latter's work at the Second Council of Constantinople in 553, and which led to the virtual eclipse of Theodore's writings after that.

In his approach to the Old Testament, Cyril was guided by two essential principles. The first was that it was a historical record of events that had to be taken seriously, not allegorized away as Origen and others might have done. The second was that it was a revelation, usually in the form of prophecy, of eternal truths that were eventually revealed in Christ. It was therefore legitimate to seek to find Christ in and under the text. On the whole, these two principles combined to form what we now call "typology." That is to say that historical events foreshadowed the coming of Christ, which was the key to interpreting them correctly.

In the New Testament, Cyril saw that the texts were deeply theological in meaning. That was not a new idea of his, of course, but he systematized his approach to a degree that had previously been unusual and generally unknown. Whereas earlier writers quoted particular verses in support of their theological arguments, Cyril wrote line-by-line commentaries linking those verses together in what came close to a systematic presentation of Christian teaching. We should not exaggerate here—he did not turn the Gospels into treatises of systematic theology as we would understand that today. Nevertheless, he had a clear idea of the presence of various theological themes that the Gospel writers and Paul developed, and he interpreted them accordingly. He did not have chapter and verse divisions in the modern sense, but he did subdivide the texts along thematic lines and treated each section or "chapter" in light of that.[5] To get an idea of this, look at the following divisions of John's Gospel:

Book 1	John 1:1–28	28 verses
Book 2	John 1:29–5:34	172 verses
Book 3	John 5:35–6:37	50 verses
Book 4	John 6:38–7:24	58 verses
Book 5	John 7:25–8:43	71 verses
Book 6	John 8:44–10:17	74 verses
Book 7	John 10:18–12:2 (fragments)	84 verses
Book 8	John 12:3–12:48 (fragments)	46 verses
Book 9	John 12:49–14:20	60 verses
Book 10	John 14:21–16:13	51 verses
Book 11	John 16:14–18:23	69 verses
Book 12	John 18:24–21:25	115 verses

It will be seen from the above that the commentary is almost completely preserved, with the exception of books 7 and 8, but the verses covered by each book vary enormously in length. This reflects Cyril's theological perceptions. The first chapter of the Gospel, which contains the famous prologue, is treated at great length because that is where the relationship between the Son (Logos or Word of God) is most clearly expounded, and it is those verses that the Arians in particular debated most fiercely. John 1 does not figure so prominently in the Nicene-Constantinopolitan Creed, where the Christological section is more dependent on Hebrews, but Cyril showed that it is absolutely central to trinitarian doctrine. Later on, he went into similar detail in the chapters dealing with the Holy Spirit, which were also vital in establishing his divinity and equality with the Father and the Son.

Cyril and the Jews

This emphasis on doctrine did not, however, make Cyril indifferent to the human touches that the fourth Gospel contains. To appreciate this properly, it is useful to take one episode, like the encounter of Jesus with Nicodemus in John 3, as illustrative of his overall approach. Modern readers may feel sympathy for Nicodemus, because although he was a Pharisee, he showed some awareness of Jesus that set him apart from others. But that is not how Cyril saw him. In Cyril's day, Alexandria had a large and active Jewish community that was strongly opposed to Christianity and said so. Cyril could not understand how educated Jews of his time were unable to perceive that their Scriptures were messianic prophecies that were fulfilled in Christ, especially since less favored Gentiles saw that immediately.

His only explanation for this was that people like Nicodemus were double-minded. On the one hand, they knew that Jesus was somehow special, but at the same time, they did not want to be upstaged as community leaders and interpreters of God's Word. Nicodemus knew the truth in his heart, but he could not break with his own people. As Cyril puts it, "Nicodemus was quite prepared to believe [in Jesus] but since he was overcome by an unhealthy regard for others and did not ignore their opinions, he refused to be straightforward and divided his mind in two. . . . Thinking that he could preserve his reputation with the Jews and still be a secret believer, he co-opted the darkness of night for his scheming . . . by coming in secret, he showed how double-minded he was."[6]

But Nicodemus's real problem was spiritual. Like other Jews, Arians, and even Nestorians (at a slightly later date), he approached Jesus as a man because that is the way that Jesus appeared to them. Like other misguided people, Nicodemus was ready to acknowledge Jesus as a man who had come from God, but no more than that. They maybe knew that Jesus was not just another prophet, but his true identity escaped them because they could not understand such deep spiritual things. Jesus therefore tells Nicodemus straight out that he cannot understand the things of God because he has not been born again of the Holy Spirit. That was a dimension of reality that was totally foreign to Nicodemus. All he could think about was the absurd idea that a man might somehow return to his mother's womb and go through the process of physical birth all over again. On this, Cyril comments, "Nicodemus thought that so high and illustrious a mystery was foolishness . . . and he tried to measure divine things without transcending the law of our [human] nature . . . just as objects hurled against dry rocks bounce back again, so an ignorant mind, when it strikes ideas more vigorous than its own, bounces back down, exhausted. And since such a mind always prefers to dwell within its own limits, it rejects the better and higher understanding. This is what happened to this ruler of the Jews, and he did not receive the [necessary] spiritual birth."[7]

Jesus then embarked on a long discourse in which he made use of material things like water and wind to explain spiritual realities. As Cyril explains, "Since Nicodemus did not understand what being born again from above means, Jesus instructed him with clearer teaching. . . . He called rebirth through the Spirit 'from above,' showing that the Spirit is a substance that is higher than anything else and that through him we become partakers of the divine nature. . . . As we enjoy the One who proceeds from the divine nature substantially, we are transformed through him and in him to the primordial beauty, and in this way we are reborn into newness of life and remade into divine sonship."[8] That this rebirth is accomplished by water and the Spirit is a reminder that our bodies are cleansed by material water just as our souls are born again by the indwelling Spirit of God. The bodily cleansing is of course symbolic of the spiritual reality, not equivalent to it, but it's given to us as material creatures so that we may better understand spiritual things.

Throughout this discourse, Nicodemus persists in his ignorance—he cannot understand the true meaning of what Jesus is talking about. The subtext is critical of him for that—as a teacher in Israel, Nicodemus should have known what Jesus was saying, but he did not. As this dialogue runs into ever deeper incomprehension, Jesus points to himself and says simply that Nicodemus should trust him, because he is the Man who has come down from heaven—a clear statement that he was not a human being exalted by God, but God who condescended to become a man. Having made this point, Jesus then goes on to cite the incident of the bronze serpent that Moses held up to the people of Israel when they were plagued by snake bites in the desert. In Cyril's words:

> God commanded Moses to raise up a bronze serpent and by doing that he ordered them to rehearse [the message of] salvation by faith. The medicine for those bitten was to look at the serpent put before them, and faith added to that vision worked deliverance for those who saw it. That is the historical narrative. By this act, he described the whole mystery of the incarnation typologically. The snake signifies bitter and murderous sin that kept feeding on the entire human race . . . the only way to escape it was through help from heaven alone. So God the Word came to be "in the likeness of sinful flesh in order to condemn sin in the flesh." He came to offer indestructible salvation to those who gaze on him with a more intent faith.[9]

Here we see clearly how Cyril interpreted the historical event in a way that gave it a spiritual meaning, not only for Nicodemus but for everyone who turns to Christ. This is how Cyril used the

Bible and how he meant it to be read and applied by believers everywhere.

Cyril's Relevance Today

What can a fifth-century bishop who was mired in controversy during his lifetime have to say to us today? It would be easy to pass over Cyril in silence, and in recent times many have done so, arguing that circumstances have changed and that there is little to be gained by trying to grasp the finer points of arguments that delve into mysteries beyond human understanding. But how wrong such an analysis would be!

Cyril showed that what we believe about God and Christ is coherent in itself and directly relevant to our spiritual lives. It is not enough to believe that Jesus was a good teacher, a great thinker, a kind man, or whatever else one might wish to say about him. Millions of people would agree with statements like these, but they are inadequate. Jesus is who and what he is because he is God in human flesh, the divine person who suffered and died for our salvation. Failure to see that is failure to understand the gospel—a message that needs to be repeated over and over again in our woolly-headed age.

Cyril also showed that the Bible is more than just a historical record of what happened long ago. It is a divine message of salvation that is as relevant today as when it was first given. Furthermore, he showed that unless we are born again in Christ, we will never see the kingdom of God. Jesus is the way, the truth, and the life—without him, nobody can ever come to the Father or dwell with him in eternity.

Cyril still reminds us that theological controversy can never be an end in itself. Its purpose is to clarify the truth about God revealed to us in Scripture and to draw us closer to him. This inevitably means saying yes to some things and no to others. Not everyone will like that, and we must take care to speak the truth in love. But speak the truth we must, and we must also remember that our foundation is the Word of God—the Logos incarnate in Christ and the message revealed in the Bible. They are one and the same, and taken together they are the key to eternal life.

● REFLECTION QUESTIONS ●

1. How important is it to define our terms precisely when engaging in theological discussion? To what extent did misunderstanding contribute to the division between Cyril and Nestorius?

2. Is it right to use individual Bible verses to make theological points, or should they always be read in context and interpreted as part of a systematic whole?

● FURTHER READING ●

Translated Texts of Cyril of Alexandria

Hill, Robert C., trans. *Commentary on Isaiah*. By Cyril of Alexandria. Holy Cross Orthodox Press, 2008.

Hill, Robert C., trans. *Commentary on the Twelve Prophets*. 3 vols. By Cyril of Alexandria. Catholic University of America Press, 2007–2008.

King, Daniel, trans. *Three Christological Treatises*. By Cyril of Alexandria. Catholic University of America Press, 2014.

Maxwell, David R., trans. *Commentary on John*. 2 vols. By Cyril of Alexandria. InterVarsity Press, 2013–2015.

Maxwell, David R., trans. *Commentaries on Romans, 1–2 Corinthians, and Hebrews*. By Cyril of Alexandria. InterVarsity Press, 2022.

McGuckin, John A., trans. *On the Unity of Christ*. By Cyril of Alexandria. St. Vladimir's Seminary Press, 1995.

Wickham, Lionel R., trans. *Select Letters*. By Cyril of Alexandria. Clarendon Press, 1983.

Studies

Farag, Lois M. *St. Cyril of Alexandria, a New Testament Exegete: His Commentary on the Gospel of John.* Gorgias Press, 2007.

Keating, Daniel A. *The Appropriation of Divine Life in Cyril of Alexandria.* Oxford University Press, 2004.

McGuckin, John A. *Saint Cyril of Alexandria and the Christological Controversy.* St. Vladimir's Seminary Press, 2004.

Ondrey, Hauna T. *The Minor Prophets as Christian Scripture in the Commentaries of Theodore of Mopsuestia and Cyril of Alexandria.* Oxford University Press, 2018.

Van Loon, Hansvan. *The Dyophysite Christology of Cyril of Alexandria.* Brill, 2009.

Weinandy, Thomas G., and Daniel A. Keating. *The Theology of St. Cyril of Alexandria: A Critical Appreciation.* T&T Clark, 2003.

Wessel, Susan. *Cyril of Alexandria and the Nestorian Controversy: The Making of a Saint and of a Heretic.* Oxford University Press, 2004.

10

THEODORET
OF CYRRHUS

(ca. AD 393–458 or 466)

Who He Was

Born about 393, Theodoret became bishop of Cyrrhus (also spelled Cyrus or Cyr), a Syrian town not far from Antioch in 423. He is said to have remained there for thirty-five years, but after 453 he disappears from the historical record. When he died is unknown, but most modern scholars guess it was before 466 at the latest.

Theodoret was a prominent citizen of Cyrrhus and used his wealth to construct great public works, including an aqueduct and an irrigation canal. He was a native Syriac speaker, but his education was thoroughly Greek, which is also the language he wrote in. We do not know whether he studied under Theodore of Mopsuestia or what his connection with Nestorius was, but he certainly moved in circles connected with them and defended them against the attacks of Cyril of Alexandria. He first came to wider attention when he reacted to

181

the twelve anathemas that Cyril attached to Pope Celestine I's condemnation of Nestorius in 430. His treatise in defense of Nestorius has been lost, but the gist of it has been preserved elsewhere, and it established Theodoret as Cyril's leading theological opponent.

Theodoret attended the First Council of Ephesus in 431, where he sided with the church of Antioch in opposition to Cyril, whom he suspected of covert Apollinarianism. After Nestorius was condemned, he wrote a lengthy treatise disputing the council's decision. When Cyril reached out to Antioch to try to achieve a reconciliation, Theodoret is said to have composed a statement of faith that he expected Cyril to sign, allowing for the orthodoxy of a "two natures" Christology. Cyril agreed to this Formula of Reunion, as it was known, but Theodoret refused to countersign it because it maintained the condemnation of Nestorius. Only when that was dropped did he relent and agree to the terms that he himself had apparently devised.

The Council of Chalcedon

An uneasy peace between Alexandria and Antioch, which was more sympathetic to the Nestorians, was maintained until Cyril died in 444, but his successor in Alexandria, a man called Dioscorus, soon opened the wounds once more. Dioscorus rejected any idea that the incarnate Christ had two natures, and a few years later one of his clergy, a man called Eutyches, went to Constantinople, where he lectured on the subject, claiming now that the humanity of Christ had been absorbed into his divinity and had no distinct existence at all. That was too much for many people, and the controversy led to a second Council of Ephesus in 449, where the Eutychian interpretation of Cyril was forced through by shutting opponents out of the debating chamber. This was a scandal, and the matter was referred once more to Rome, where Pope Leo I (440–461) issued a statement known as his *Tome*, which was meant to resolve the dispute once and for all.[1]

182

Leo basically agreed with Cyril's theology but used some Nestorian-sounding terms to refine it. In particular, he insisted that the incarnate Christ had two natures after the union—as Nestorius had done—but that they were joined by a single (divine) *hypostasis*—as Cyril would have insisted. Following Latin usage, Leo called this *hypostasis* the *persona* of Christ, thereby making *hypostasis* and *persona* (*prosōpon* in Greek) synonymous, something that had not been generally accepted before.

The equation of *persona* and *hypostasis* owes its origin to the problem of translating Greek theological terms into Latin. The first man to do this was Tertullian, writing around 200. Tertullian translated *ousia* ("being") not as *essentia*, which would have been the exact equivalent, but as *substantia*. That was possible because in his day *hypostasis*, which is the Greek equivalent of *substantia*, was still being used in the sense of "being," and the Romans found it more natural than *essentia*, which struck them as an artificial construct. This, however, made it impossible for Tertullian to use *substantia* to refer to the Father, Son, and Holy Spirit as three distinct identities, since he could hardly say they were three substances in the one substance without causing confusion.

In order to supply this need, Tertullian turned to the word *persona*. Originally it had just been a translation of *prosōpon* and was used to mean "mask" in the theater. But unlike the Greek word, it developed along different lines. It was taken over by Roman law and used to mean someone who could litigate in the courts, which had their own form of drama, as it were. A *persona* thus became an adult male Roman citizen, but it could also be used for a registered company, which acquired what we call "legal personality" by being "incorporated" ("embodied"). We are still familiar with this usage today.

The important thing to bear in mind is that a *persona* was an agent who could do things, whereas a *hypostasis* was an identity—something that could be observed but that was not necessarily active. Furthermore, although *persona* was the Latin equivalent of *prosōpon*, it was not what Nestorius meant by that term. For the Nestorians, the *prosōpon* of Christ was the *result* of the incarnation, whereas for Leo, it was the *cause* of it, making it much more like Cyril's *hypostasis*.

But where Cyril's *hypostasis* was the concrete manifestation of the Son's underlying divine "being" (*ousia*), from which it could not be detached, Leo's *persona* of the Son was a divine agent that was more than that. His *persona* could reach out beyond his "being" (*substantia* or *ousia*) and become the governing principle of another "being"—in this case, the humanity of Jesus formed in the womb of Mary. In this way the one divine *persona* of the Son could have two complete natures (*naturae* or *physeis*), incompatible with each other but joined by sharing a common *hypostasis*. In other words, *persona* and *hypostasis* were the same thing, and in the incarnate Christ the *persona* of the Son possessed two natures, each of which functioned according to its own principles without being confused with the other.

This formula—one divine *hypostasis* or *persona* in two natures (*physeis*) was adopted by the Council of Chalcedon in 451 and became the accepted orthodoxy of the Western (Latin) and half the Eastern (Greek) churches, which it still is.[2] If you are Roman Catholic, Protestant, or Eastern Orthodox today, then you are a Chalcedonian Christian, whether you realize it or not!

Cyril did not live long enough to be confronted with the Chalcedonian solution. Would he have accepted it? This is the great unanswerable question. Modern Chalcedonians argue that Cyril's teaching was substantially the same as that of the council, that Cyril would have agreed to it once he understood that the word *physis* caused confusion if it was used in two different senses, and that a different way of expressing what he wanted to say was necessary. They point out that Cyril accepted that a "two natures" formula was possible in certain circumstances, because the human nature was not simply absorbed into the divine, and so there should have been no problem in accepting it. On the other hand, the Chalcedonians tend to downplay the fact that Cyril preferred to use the "one nature" formula and thought of the "two natures" formula as an essentially political concession to the Nestorians. That is certainly what Cyril's successors thought, and it is not unreasonable to suppose that they were in a position to know.

Whatever the truth of the matter, the Chalcedonian and non-Chalcedonian churches drew apart, and although there have been occasional attempts to reunite the Monophysites of Alexandria with the Chalcedonians, no reunion has ever been achieved. Chalcedon marked a turning point in discussions about the nature of Christ's humanity, but it did not solve every problem. For example, it did not decide whether Jesus had one will or two. If he had only one, it would necessarily have been divine, but if he did not have a human will, could he have been a human like us? Did the will belong to Christ's person (*hypostasis*) or to his natures? It was eventually decided that he had two wills, since otherwise a verse like Matthew 26:39 would make no sense. In his prayer in the garden of Gethsemane, Jesus asked that he be spared the crucifixion but concluded by submitting his (human) will to that of the Father. If he had possessed only a divine will, it would have been that of the Father, and his "submission" of one to the other would have been inconceivable.[3] The issue was not finally resolved until the Third Council of Constantinople in 680 to 681, more than two centuries after Chalcedon, which puts the latter's achievements in proper historical perspective. Chalcedon was not the end of the process, and it would be a long time before its legacy was fully understood, even by those who supported it in principle, but after 451 there could be no going back.

Theodoret and Chalcedon

Theodoret went to the Council of Chalcedon but encountered considerable opposition from many of the other bishops there. He was not allowed into the council's first seven sessions, during which Eutyches and Dioscorus, Cyril's successor as bishop of Alexandria, were both deposed. The assembled bishops then took Theodoret aside and examined his writings, but they insisted that he denounce Nestorius before they would allow him to take up his seat. Theodoret resisted this pressure as long as he could, but in the end he complied and was reinstated.

His conversion to Chalcedonian orthodoxy, though hardly voluntary, seems to have been sincere and represented his willingness to accept the definition of Christ's two natures, which the council decreed were united "without confusion, without change, without division, and without separation."[4] The first two of these definitions were aimed against the Apollinarians and the last two against the Nestorians, but Theodoret managed to interpret them according to his own basically Antiochene Christology. It seems that his fundamental approach changed very little, but he was able to finesse his principles just enough to be considered orthodox by Chalcedonian standards.

The rest of Theodoret's life passed in obscurity, and we do not even know whether he returned to Cyrrhus after the council or not. A century later, in 553, as part of an attempt to reconcile Chalcedonians and the Monophysite followers of Cyril, his anti-Cyrillian works were condemned by the Second Council of Constantinople, though he himself was spared because he had signed the Chalcedonian Definition. As a result, most of his writings have been preserved in the original Greek, and we have a precious witness to how a theologian trained in the school of Antioch could accommodate a way of thinking that was fundamentally different from his own.

Theodoret's Writings

Theodoret was a prolific writer. His exegetical works include collections of questions on the Old Testament from Genesis to 2 Chronicles, in which he tried to answer difficulties posed by the texts. He also wrote full-length commentaries on the Psalter, the Song of Songs, Isaiah, Jeremiah, Ezekiel, Daniel, the Minor Prophets, and, in his only foray into the New Testament, the fourteen epistles of Paul (including Hebrews). In addition to those, he also wrote numerous theological treatises, of which the most important was his *Eranistes*, which was written just before the Eutychian controversy erupted and survives intact. It is a comprehensive refutation of Monophysitism as Theodoret understood it.

As if that were not enough, Theodoret also composed an *Ecclesiastical History* that was designed to complement the one written by Eusebius of Caesarea more than a century before, as well as other historical works that concentrated on the rise of monasticism and the development of different heresies. Finally, Theodoret tackled the still active pagan Neoplatonists, whom he attempted to discredit, and the Jews who remained influential and were still proselytizing Christians in Syria and the East generally. Few church fathers had as broad a range of interests as Theodoret had, and the survival of most of his writings gives us a picture of the intellectual state of the church at the time of the Council of Chalcedon that we would not otherwise possess.

For a long time, many of his writings were lost or else circulated under the names of others, making it difficult to decide what he really thought about the controversies he was engaged in. Painstaking research in the twentieth century and the happy rediscovery of some important treatises—most notably his commentary on Isaiah—have made it possible to reconstruct a plausible intellectual biography of him, but he remains a relatively understudied and neglected figure, despite his obvious importance.[5]

How Theodoret Read the Bible

Like others of his time, Theodoret wrote extensively on the Bible, though most of his commentaries appeared in the interval between the Councils of Ephesus (431) and Chalcedon (451). For the most part they say little or nothing about Nestorius or the ideas associated with him, but concentrate almost exclusively on Arianism, which Theodoret regarded as the archetypal Alexandrian heresy, and its offshoot Apollinarianism. Various explanations have been given for this, the most plausible being that he did not want to fall under the ban pronounced against Nestorius in 431 by being too openly supportive of his views. If that is true, it was a wise precaution to take, and in any case, it is not difficult to reconstruct his affinities with the Nestorian point of view, which come out clearly in his opposition to the Arians and Apollinarians.

Theodoret approached the Scriptures in the hope of resolving the Christological disputes of his time by uncovering what they really said about the incarnate Christ. To appreciate this properly, we must keep in mind that both he and his opponents held a number of principles in common and were trying to express them in a coherent and noncontradictory way. The basic points of agreement can be set out as follows:

1. Divinity is incapable of suffering.
2. In the death and resurrection of Jesus, it was his humanity that suffered and died, not his divinity.
3. Every aspect of human nature was present on the cross, and so the entire human being was redeemed by Christ's atoning sacrifice.

The points at issue were:

1. Was there a sense in which it could be said that God suffered and died on the cross, even though divinity was incapable of experiencing those things? The Alexandrians said that the *hypostasis* of the Word (Logos) of God suffered and died in the human nature he assumed in the womb of Mary. The Antiochenes preferred to say that the Word assumed a human being in Mary's womb and

that it was he, and not the Word, who suffered and died. But at the same time, they rejected the idea that there were two Sons, one divine and the other human. How could God and man be two *hypostases* in Christ without there being two Sons, since each *hypostasis* would have to be the subject of its own actions? Was such a solution viable?

2. If divinity shared in the suffering of Christ in some respect, was it really divinity? Did such a concept not diminish the fullness of the Son's Godhead and make him no more than a creature like us—divine in some sense, perhaps, but not uniquely God?

3. Could the Son of God be a real substitute for sinful human beings on the cross if his humanity was not a distinct identity (*hypostasis*) of its own? Even if the parts of human nature assumed by the Son amounted to 100 percent of the whole, without a *hypostasis* could those assembled parts be considered a "man"?

These were the questions that Theodoret brought to his reading of the Bible, and he read with the expectation that it would give him the answers, but it would be wrong to suggest that he twisted his interpretation of the Scriptures in order to fit his preconceived ideas. Theodoret was willing to be corrected by what they had to say, and the evidence of his commentaries and later theological treatises suggests that he actually was—at least to the extent of being able to sign the Chalcedonian Definition as a true statement of what the Bible teaches about the incarnate Christ.

The Disciple of Theodore of Mopsuestia

When we look at Theodoret's Old Testament commentaries, his debt to Theodore of Mopsuestia is immediately apparent. Like Theodore, Theodoret eschewed allegory as much as possible and emphasized the primacy of history as the key to interpreting the text. He believed that the prophets had spoken to their contemporaries in a way that was meaningful to them, and he did not insist that every Old Testament passage had a direct application to the future coming of Christ. Like Theodore, he sometimes allowed this approach to distract him from those New Testament passages that interpreted the Hebrew Bible in metaphorical and messianic terms, though he was more flexible than Theodore had been in allowing for the possibility of typology in the prophetic writings. This made him more willing to accept Alexandrian interpretations of the same passages and facilitated an understanding between the two traditions that would not have been possible with Theodore. In the end, this flexibility allowed Theodoret to appreciate Cyril's Christology and that of the Council of Chalcedon enough for him to be able to sign its documents and to be counted as orthodox, though his underlying approach and general attitude remained firmly Antiochene in orientation.

Theodoret was also more willing than Theodore to find figurative interpretations for the literal sense of the Scriptures, but he regarded such meanings as extensions of the literal sense and not as substitutes for it. He did not reject some Old Testament passages on the grounds that they were unworthy of Christian thinking or treat them as no longer relevant to the Christian life and instead did his best to apply them in changed circumstances.

For example, he dismissed Theodore's belief that the Song of Songs was a bridal hymn composed by Solomon for his Egyptian wife and accepted that it was intended to be read metaphorically from the beginning, a view that he shared with virtually every other Christian commentator and a number of Jewish ones as well. But he did not hesitate to punctuate his commentaries with occasional asides designed to encourage his congregations to find ways of relating such metaphors to their own circumstances, especially to their own relationship with God. There is a strong pastoral note in his exegesis, which is one reason why it proved to be so popular with later generations who were looking for pastoral guidance and not just historical information.

As an example of his approach, consider what he says at the end of his commentary on Psalm 147: "What has been said is enough to explain the literal sense. If you want to take the psalm in a figurative sense as well, we shall not object, without doing violence to the historical meaning but adding the figurative one to the extent that it is appropriate."[6] This dual emphasis was typical of Theodoret's Old Testament exegesis, though there were occasions when he went much further in the direction of a metaphorical interpretation. For example, in his commentary on Daniel 2:34, which speaks of a stone that was cut out of a mountain without human hands being used, Theodoret was at great pains to say that this was a reference to Christ. As he puts it: "We learn from the Old and New Testament that our Lord Jesus Christ was called a stone. It was cut from a mountain without hands being used, being born of a virgin independently of marital intercourse."[7] Theodoret could reach such a conclusion because of the numerous references in both Testaments to "a stone of stumbling" and the rock that followed the people in the desert, which the apostle Paul said was Christ (1 Pet. 2:8).[8]

Theodoret believed that the Scriptures were authored by the Holy Spirit and that they could therefore be strung together as revelations of a single divine reality, which manifested itself in different historical circumstances but was essentially the same in every case. This allowed him greater freedom of interpretation than would have been possible for Theodore of Mopsuestia, as for example in his explanation of Psalm 55:4–5. Commenting on the graphic description of the terrors of death mentioned in those verses, he refers them to the human nature that Christ assumed in the incarnation: "It was necessary for the nature that suffered to be revealed, as well as the extraordinary patience that the loving God had for our human race. [Christ] underwent suffering in the flesh, wishing in this to be involved in our salvation."[9]

It was by this kind of detailed exegesis that Theodoret came to appreciate the Alexandrian insistence that it was the Son of God who suffered and died in his human nature and that while that nature was not absorbed into his divinity (as Eutyches maintained), it did not have its own *hypostasis* distinct from that of the Word (Logos) either. Reading the Bible in this way brought Theodoret closer to Chalcedon than he would have been otherwise and paved the way for him to accept the "one divine Person in two natures" Christology that the council consecrated as orthodox. Modern readers may think he chose a roundabout way to get there, but in his own terms Theodoret was able to transcend the obvious limitations of his inherited two-natures Christology and to distance himself from the Nestorians. Intellectual humility of that kind is rare in theologians, who usually try to bend the biblical text to suit their preconceived ideas rather than submit to its teaching, and in this respect Theodoret must be recognized for the great mind that he was.

Rediscovering Theodoret

Does Theodoret have anything to say to us today? He has been neglected over the years and is still little known, even in professional theological circles. Is that a fair assessment of his work, or is there something more to be said?

Theodoret is still important to us because he insisted on the importance of the historical underpinnings of the biblical narrative. The history of salvation is not a myth, nor is it a biased account written to suit the prejudices of a later age. It is the story of real events that happened to real people and that were recorded as prophecies of the Christ who was to come. We take the Old Testament as seriously as we do partly because we share Theodoret's perspective on this.

Theodoret is a model for theologians of every age because he was prepared to submit his own beliefs to the judgment of Scripture.

He was deeply attached to men like Theodore of Mopsuestia and Nestorius, but when he realized that their interpretation of the Bible was inadequate, he moved on from them and was not afraid to align himself with positions that he had previously repudiated. This willingness to be persuaded by the evidence is all too rare in human life, and we must admire Theodoret for it.

Theodoret continues to challenge us because of the way he kept theological disagreements in perspective. Although he recognized the limitations of his friends and mentors, he was not prepared to turn against them in the way others insisted that he should. He understood that they had been sincere seekers after the truth and continued to respect them for that, even as he later disagreed with them. This charity and loyalty did not prevent him from moving on to a more nuanced understanding of Christology, but these qualities survived at a personal level. Too often theological debates leave broken relationships in their wake and make it impossible to achieve any kind of reconciliation. Theodoret could not work miracles in that respect, but neither did he make the situation worse by attacking his old friends in a way that would have been unfair to them. It is a balance we can all learn from, and Theodoret should be recognized for the great pastor and reconciler he turned out to be.

● REFLECTION QUESTIONS ●

1. In defending our faith, when is it right to stick to established terms and formulations, and when can we consider the possibility of going beyond them?

2. Is it possible to reconcile fundamentally opposing points of view, or does one eventually have to give way to the other? Are compromises ever possible where fundamental truths are concerned?

● FURTHER READING ●

Translated Texts of Theodoret

Bray, Gerald L., trans. *Commentary on Isaiah*. By Theodoret. Inter-Varsity, 2026.

Ettlinger, Gerard H., trans. *Eranistes*. By Theodoret. Catholic University of America Press, 2003.

Hill, Robert C., trans. *Commentary on Daniel*. By Theodoret. Society of Biblical Literature Press, 2006.

Hill, Robert C., trans. *Commentary on Ezekiel*. By Theodoret. Holy Cross Orthodox Press, 2006.

Hill, Robert C., trans. *Commentary on the Letters of St. Paul*. 2 vols. By Theodoret. Holy Cross Orthodox Press, 2001.

Hill, Robert C., trans. *Commentary on the Psalms*. 2 vols. By Theodoret. Catholic University of America Press, 2000–2001.

Hill, Robert C., trans. *Commentary on the Song of Songs*. By Theodoret. Australian Catholic University Press, 2001.

Hill, Robert C., trans. *Commentary on the Twelve Prophets*. By Theodoret. Holy Cross Orthodox Press, 2006.

Hill, Robert C., trans. *The Questions on the Octateuch*. By Theodoret. Catholic University of America Press, 2007.

Studies

Clayton, Paul B., Jr. *The Christology of Theodoret of Cyrus: Antiochene Christology from the Council of Ephesus (431) to the Council of Chalcedon (451)*. Oxford University Press, 2007.

Hill, Robert C. *Reading the Old Testament in Antioch*. Society of Biblical Literature Press, 2005.

Pásztori-Kupán, István. *Theodoret of Cyrus*. Routledge, 2006.

Siniossoglou, Niketas. *Plato and Theodoret: The Christian Appropriation of Platonic Philosophy and the Hellenic Intellectual Resistance*. Cambridge University Press, 2008.

Vranic, Vasilije. *The Constancy and Development in the Christology of Theodoret of Cyrrhus*. Brill, 2015.

Wallace-Hadrill, D. S. *Christian Antioch: A Study of Early Christian Thought in the East*. Cambridge University Press, 1982.

Conclusion

When the Pharisees confronted Jesus about his teaching, he replied, "You search the Scriptures because you think that in them you have eternal life; and it is they that bear witness about me" (John 5:39). The first followers of Jesus took his words to heart. Like the Pharisees and other Jews of their time, they took the Bible as their guide to spiritual truth, and in it they found the portrait of Jesus Christ, as he told them they would. They did not deny that the Old Testament was the historical legacy of ancient Israel, the law given to Moses and the prophets by which God's people were called to live. But in that law, as Jesus taught them, they saw the promise of a future fulfillment of God's message of salvation that would be proclaimed to the ends of the earth. That message was not a law or a philosophy but a person—the Son of God who came into the world in order to suffer and die for our sins and, by his resurrection from the dead, to open the kingdom of heaven to all believers.

Those early followers walked in the footsteps of the men who were on the road to Emmaus immediately after Jesus's crucifixion and before they fully understood the resurrection. Jesus came up alongside them incognito and began to expound the Bible to them, showing them how what had happened had been foretold. When the penny finally dropped and they recognized him for who he was, they said to one another: "Did not our hearts burn within us while he talked to us on the road, while he opened to us the Scriptures?" (Luke 24:32).

This was the experience of the early Christians. They read the Hebrew Bible, and in it they found Jesus Christ. Sometimes this discovery was clear to them, as it was to Justin Martyr, who did not hesitate to challenge the Jews of his time to read the texts in the same way he did and to find Christ for themselves. At other times, it was more obscure, hidden behind a veil that had to be removed for the Savior's glory to be made plain. Getting beneath the surface of the text was a skill that was given to only a few, but those who received that gift made the most of it. Nobody was more consistent in this than Origen, the first person who can properly be called a systematic biblical theologian. Origen did not reject the literal sense of the Bible, but where it was not clear he went beyond it and found what he was looking for in some unlikely places. He knew that not everyone would come to the same conclusions he did, but he paved the way for others to follow, and for the rest of ancient history, he remained central to everyone's understanding of Scripture, whether they agreed with him or reacted against what they saw as his errors and excesses.

By Origen's time, the task of finding Christ in the Scriptures had been expanded to include what we now call the New Testament. Compared with the Hebrew Bible, the New Testament was crystal clear, apart from a few anomalies like the book of Revelation. Some of it was so clear, in fact, that the fathers of the church had little to say about it—the book of Acts being the outstanding example of that. It was hundreds of years before anybody wrote a commentary on that book because everyone took it at face value and felt that commentary was unnecessary.

In some places, the New Testament explained the meaning of Christ's life and death, often by showing the Old Testament prophecies that lay behind them, and in those cases the church fathers could simply expound the teaching of apostles like Paul without needing to go beyond the literal sense of the text in front of them. The commentary of the anonymous Ambrosiaster and the sermons of John Chrysostom are excellent examples of this—they had their perspectives and prejudices, to be sure, but the message was clear, and the skill with which they conveyed it has survived into modern times.

Later generations built on this inheritance and explored it still further. What exactly was the portrait of Jesus that the Bible presented? Was he a man specially blessed by God, or was he God come down to earth in human flesh? The evidence of the Bible was tossed to and fro as interpreters sought to make sense of sayings and incidents recorded in the Gospels. They were frequently at a loss for words, but eventually they came to a consensus that has stood the test of time—Jesus Christ was the Son of God, the Second Person of the Trinity of Father, Son, and Holy Spirit. He became a human in the womb of the Virgin Mary, lived a human life, died an all too human death, and rose again to a new life, the firstfruits of the salvation that he promised to his followers. Ten days after his ascension into heaven, he sent his Holy Spirit to dwell in the hearts of those who believed in him, and the church as we know it was born.

It took time to get the portrait right, and not everybody accepted the decisions that the majority of the church eventually took, but the pattern was set, and it has endured. The more adventurous fantasies of some nonliteral interpretations were sidelined, if not completely eliminated, and the writings of Augustine of Hippo and Theodoret of Cyrrhus would eventually show that there was no need for them. By the time the Council of Chalcedon met to hammer out its definition of the person of Christ, the fathers of the church could legitimately claim that what they were teaching and preaching was plain for all to see in the Scriptures. The finer points of theological detail might still need to be worked out, but the basic framework was in place, and it has continued to be received by most Christians to the present day.

The patristic age did not end in 451, but certain factors were at work in the fifth century that make it appropriate for us to conclude our study at this point. In the Latin West, the Roman Empire was on its last legs, and within a few years it had collapsed altogether. When Western Europe reemerged centuries later as an intellectual center, it was in very different circumstances, and continuity with the patristic era had been broken. Theologians of what we now call the Middle Ages looked back to the church fathers and honored their legacy, but they were conscious of belonging to a new dispensation. They had moved on.

In the Eastern Christian world, connection with the past was maintained for longer than in the West, but change was afoot there too. The post-Chalcedonian fallout produced churches that were no longer in communion with one another, and the rise of Islam cut the non-Chalcedonians off from the rest of the Christian world. The empire based in Constantinople continued to regard itself as Roman, but it was Greek-speaking and (Chalcedonian) Orthodox, a combination we now call Byzantine. It, too, was different from what had gone before.

By the late fifth century, the pagan world in which Christianity had emerged and which the church was forced to combat was in its dying throes. Pagan temples were being turned into churches, pagan ceremonies were being suppressed or Christianized, and pagan philosophies were being discounted. The closure of the philosophical schools of Athens in 529 was the final act in this drama; after that, Christianity had a monopoly in every walk of life, and the struggles of the past were increasingly forgotten.

The downside of that was that the golden age of patristic theology and literature also came to an end, as the need to defend Christian views became less pressing, and even once-popular Christian heresies were progressively sidelined and disappeared. People did not stop praying, nor did they stop thinking, but the atmosphere had changed, and with it went the particular combination of ancient and modern that had so marked the patristic era.

Choosing only ten of the major representatives of early church thought is a difficult task, because there is so much more that can be said. But if we take what mattered most to the church fathers—the use and interpretation of the Bible—the selection we have here is not unjustified. Every church father drew on the Scriptures for teaching and inspiration, but not all were as influential as the ten men featured here. They had an impact that went far beyond their own circles, and in important ways their legacy resonates with the concerns of the church today.

We live in a different time and have far more resources at our disposal than the church fathers had. It is easy for us to criticize them for weaknesses that were not apparent to them or that they could not overcome. A faith rooted in a written text is hard to maintain if reliable written texts cannot be easily reproduced, and that was a handicap that theologians had to live with until printing was invented a millennium later.

What is truly remarkable about the church fathers is the degree of consensus they managed to achieve in spite of these difficulties. For all their faults, they remain models of piety and scholarship that continue to challenge us today. Their struggles to find the best definitions of the terms needed to express the great doctrines of the Trinity and of Christ were drawn out and not entirely successful, but their achievements were nonetheless monumental, and subsequent theological developments have built on the foundations they laid. We can probe those foundations and occasionally suggest ways they might be improved, but we cannot dispense with them altogether.

In the providence of God, the church fathers represent the pathway the gospel has taken, and it will continue along the same path until Christ comes again in glory. On that day we shall see just how important the church fathers have been in the outworking of the divine plan of salvation, and we will render thanks to the God who led them, as we hope and pray that he is leading us, out of darkness into his glorious light.

Additional Resources

Altaner, Berthold, and Alfred Stuiber. *Patrologie*. 9th ed. Herder, 1978.

Blowers, Paul M. *The Oxford Handbook of Early Christian Biblical Interpretation*. Edited by Peter W. Martens. Oxford University Press, 2019.

De Cock, Miriam, and Elizabeth Klein, eds. *Patristic Exegesis in Context: Exploring the Genres of Early Christian Biblical Interpretation*. Catholic University of America Press, 2023.

Di Berardino, Angelo, ed. *Encyclopedia of Ancient Christianity*. 3 vols. InterVarsity Press, 2014.

Di Berardino, Angelo, ed. "Greek Exegetical Catenae." In *Patrology: The Eastern Fathers from the Council of Chalcedon (451) to John of Damascus (†750)*. James Clarke, 2006.

Hauser, Alan J., and Duane F. Watson. *A History of Biblical Interpretation*. Vol. 1, *The Ancient Period*. Eerdmans, 2003.

Heine, Ronald E. *Reading the Old Testament with the Ancient Church: Exploring the Formation of Early Christian Thought*. Baker, 2007.

Kannengiesser, Charles. *Handbook of Patristic Exegesis: The Bible in Ancient Christianity*. 2 vols. Brill, 2004.

Oden, Thomas C., ed. *Ancient Christian Commentary on Scripture*. InterVarsity Press, 1996–2010.

Paget, James C., and Joachim Schaper, eds. *The New Cambridge History of the Bible*. Vol. 1, *From the Beginnings to 600*. Cambridge University Press, 2013.

Quasten, Johannes. *Patrology.* 6 vols. Edited by Angelo Di Berardino. Spectrum, 1950–60; Christian Classics, 1986; Marietti, 1996; James Clarke, 2006.

Reventlow, Henning G. *History of Biblical Interpretation.* 2 vols. Society of Biblical Literature, 2009.

Toom, Tarmo, ed. *Patristic Theories of Biblical Interpretation: The Latin Fathers.* Cambridge University Press, 2016.

APPENDIX

Key Theological Terms

The history of the early church cannot be understood without some knowledge of the key theological terms that were used in debates about the Trinity and the identity of Jesus Christ. These debates were conducted in Greek, but Latin translations were soon available, and it is through them that the terms have come into most European languages, including English. The words themselves were already in existence in both languages, but they were not precise enough for the needs of Christian theology. Many of the debates that ensued concerned this problem, and the history of the period can largely be written in terms of the time and effort it took to establish an adequate vocabulary for describing the great mysteries of God revealed in Holy Scripture.

The Greek World

In Greek there were four key terms that theologians used. They were *ousia*, *hypostasis*, *physis*, and *prosōpon*.

Ousia is a noun created from the verb "to be" and can be translated as "being" in English. There is only one God, and therefore there can be only one divine *ousia*. Like God himself, it stays the same yesterday, today, and forever.

Hypostasis is a compound of *hypo-* ("under") and *stasis* ("stand") and originally meant something like "fundamental substance." In New Testament times, it was sometimes used to mean *ousia*, but this did not last long. In Hebrews 1:3 it is used to describe the Son of God as "the exact imprint of [the Father's] nature," as the ESV puts it, though this is a bad translation. Even "being" would be better than "nature" in this case, because what the writer is trying to say is that the Father and the Son are identical in "substance," though they can be distinguished at a different level, which the writer calls "character," translated here as "imprint."

Before long, the Greeks were using *hypostasis* as the word to describe the threeness of the Trinity—the Father, the Son, and the Holy Spirit were all identifiable as distinct *hypostases* in the single *ousia*.

Physis described what an *ousia* or a *hypostasis* was like. In God, the *physis* of the *ousia* and of the three *hypostases* was basically the same—invisible, immortal, impassible, incomprehensible, and so on. Because of this, the *physis* of the Son was the same as the *physis* of the divine being (*ousia*), making him fully God alongside the Father and the Holy Spirit. But both *ousia* and *physis* were essentially invisible abstractions. They could only be perceived in and through the *hypostases* or "identities" that they had. God the Father was a *hypostasis* of the divine *ousia* and its *physis*. This was also true of God the Son and of God the Holy Spirit, who both had exactly the same *ousia* and *physis* also. This is how they could all be the one God and yet be distinguishable.

In the ancient creeds of the church, we often say that Jesus Christ is "fully God and fully man," but we are liable to misunderstand what "God" and "man" are in this context. They are not separate beings somehow joined together, but different *physeis*. It would be more accurate to translate the phrase as "fully divine and fully human," though we seldom (if ever) do so.

Prosōpon was a word borrowed from ancient Greek theater, where it meant "mask." Since ancient theater was largely masked performances, the actors came to be identified by the masks they wore. From there, the word developed to mean "face" (as in, "put on a face"), and this is how it is used in the New Testament. Paul tells us that in heaven we shall see God "face to face" (1 Cor. 13:12). In English we can say the same thing with the words "person to person," but if we do, we are making it clear that *prosōpon* no longer means "mask" but the exact opposite. To know God "face to face" is to see him without a mask, though this change in meaning was not universal, nor was it really understood by most people at the time.

The Latin World

Enter the Latins. From the beginning, they translated the Greek terms and did so without paying much attention to their origins. Our English terms are usually just adaptations of the Latin ones, so translation is hardly necessary. For example, *essentia* is "essence," *substantia* is "substance," and so on.

To begin with *ousia*, it should have become *essentia*, from the Latin verb "to be" (*esse*), but the Romans did not like that word and generally avoided it. Instead, they preferred to use *substantia*, which is a direct translation of *hypostasis*. Compound words based on the Greek *ousia* were therefore normally translated by creating Latin words based on *substantia*, so that the Greek *homoousios* ("of one being") was rendered as *consubstantialis*, as it still is, rather than as *coessentialis*.

To express the three identities in the one divine *substantia*, or what the Greeks called the three *hypostases*, the Latin theologian Tertullian (ca. 160–ca. 200) came up with the word *persona*. In origin, *persona* was a translation of the Greek word *prosōpon* and was used in the same theatrical context. Even today, the cast of characters listed at the head of a play is often called the *dramatis personae*. But the Romans quickly moved from the theater to the courtroom, where a different kind of drama took place. In that context, a *persona* became somebody who could sue or be sued in litigation. Only a Roman citizen was a *persona*—women, children, and foreigners were excluded! On the other hand, a company could be given what is called "legal personality," making it possible for it to be sued in a court of law as a *persona*.

Tertullian did not hesitate to use *persona* to mean *hypostasis*, perhaps not realizing that the Greek word did not necessarily include the element of agency (or "acting") that the Latin one had acquired. It was a brilliant choice, and we still describe the Trinity as "three persons in one substance" today. Unfortunately, some Greeks mistook this use of *persona* for "mask" and accused the Latins of not believing in the Trinity at all, but of imagining that the one God played different roles in some great cosmic drama—the Father was the Creator, the Son was the Redeemer, and the Holy Spirit was the Sanctifier, as if the roles they performed determined their identity as persons. But because Greeks and Latins did not communicate with each other very much, that did not matter for a long time. Each language group went its own way and ignored the other one as much as possible.

As for *physis*, it was translated as *natura*, from *nasci* ("to be born"). Whether the divine *personae* had the same *natura* as the divine *substantia* did not particularly trouble the Latins, who were not as philosophically minded as the Greeks, and it faded into the background as a distinct theological term. For our purposes, *natura* applies equally to both, and God's nature is the same, whether we are speaking about his *substantia* or his *personae*.

Notes

Before We Begin

1. See Matthew 28:19–20.
2. It should be said that we are not really consistent either. For the most part we have accepted the order of the Old Testament books and their names from the Greek, even though the text is translated directly from the Hebrew. Breaking with the patristic (and medieval) tradition is harder than it might seem.
3. For a detailed examination of that particular question, see Andrew J. Brown, *Recruiting the Ancients for the Creation Debate* (Eerdmans, 2023).

Chapter 1 Justin Martyr

1. Justin Martyr, *First Apology* 44.9–10.
2. Justin, *First Apology* 32.2.
3. Justin, *First Apology* 32.4.
4. Justin, *First Apology* 33.1, 33.5, 34.1.
5. See Matthew 1:20–21; 2:6; Luke 1:31–32.
6. Justin, *First Apology* 66.3. Justin never quoted John's Gospel directly, but in his *Dialogue with Trypho* (105.1) he referred to Christ as the "only-begotten" Son of the Father, indicating that he may have known John 1:14, where that phrase is used.
7. This may have been the hypothetical Q (for "Quelle"), the existence of which is controversial among New Testament scholars.
8. In *Dialogue with Trypho* 39.4, Justin quotes Psalm 68:18, "He ascended on high, he led captivity captive and gave gifts to men," which Paul also quoted in Ephesians 4:8. Did Justin get this from Paul? Perhaps—we do not know.
9. See Luke 24:27.

10. The Septuagint is so called from the Latin word *septuaginta*, which means "seventy," because legend had it that it was translated from Hebrew by seventy (or perhaps seventy-two) Jewish rabbis. It was composed in stages from about 275 BC until the time of Jesus but was of uneven quality and was being replaced. in Justin's day by more accurate versions.

11. Justin Martyr, *Dialogue with Trypho* 66.2.

12. Justin, *Dialogue* 111.2.

13. Isaiah 7:14 is quoted in *First Apology* 33.1 and in *Dialogue with Trypho* 43.5–6, 66.2–3, 68.6, 71.3, and 84.1. Isaiah 53 is quoted wholly or in part in *First Apology* 50.2, 51.1–5, and 54.8. It is also quoted in *Dialogue with Trypho* 14.8, 32.1, 32.2, 36.6, 42.2, 43.3, 49.2, 63.2, 68.4, 72.3, 76.2, 85.1, 89.3, 90.1, 95.3, 97.2, 102.7, 111.3, 114.2, 116.3, 126.1, and 137.1.

14. Justin, *Dialogue* 77.2–4.

15. Justin, *Dialogue* 41.1–3, 42.1.

16. Justin, *Dialogue* 111.4. See Joshua 2:18.

17. Justin, *Dialogue* 56. See Genesis 18:1–14.

18. Justin, *Dialogue* 58.6. See Genesis 32:22–32.

19. Justin, *Dialogue* 59. See Exodus 3:4–22.

20. Jeremiah 31:31–32. Quoted in Justin, *Dialogue* 11.3.

21. Justin, *Dialogue* 11.5. There's a clear echo here of Romans 4:9–10.

22. Justin, *Dialogue* 29.2–3.

23. Justin, *Dialogue* 32.1.

24. Justin, *Dialogue* 13.2–9, 97.3–105.1, 114.2.

25. Justin, *Dialogue* 33.1–34.6.

26. Justin, *Dialogue* 52.4. See also 110.5.

27. Justin, *Dialogue* 35.2. See 35.1–5.

28. Justin, *Dialogue* 142.3.

Chapter 2 Origen

1. For example, he suggested that John 1:28 should read "Betharaba" instead of "Bethany." Origen, *Commentary on John* 6.204–205, 212–214.

2. Origen, *Homilies on Leviticus* 1.1.

3. Origen, *First Principles* 1.pref.1; Origen, *Homilies on Isaiah* 1.5; Origen, *Commentary on Matthew* 28.54.119; Origen, *Fragments on John* 46.

4. Origen, *First Principles* 4.1–3. He cites Genesis 49:10, Deuteronomy 32:21, Psalm 45:1–2, and Isaiah 7:14 as examples.

5. Origen, *Leviticus* 1.1. This idea can be found in the Bible itself and was not an invention of Origen's. See 2 Corinthians 3:15, referring to Exodus 34:29–35.

6. Origen, *First Principles* 1.pref.8, 1.3.1, 4.2.7, 4.3.14.

7. Origen, *First Principles* 4.2.7; Origen, *Against Celsus* 3.45, 5.29; Origen, *Commentary on the Song of Songs* 3.218. See Matthew 7:6.

8. See 1 Corinthians 2:10.

9. Origen, *John* 13.305.

10. Origen, *Leviticus* 1.3; Origen, *Matthew* 10.9.

11. Origen, *Homilies on Numbers* 1.3; Origen, *Homilies on Joshua* 1.4, 2.1; Origen, *John* 32.341. See Galatians 3:24–27.

12. Origen, *Leviticus* 6.2; Origen, *Joshua* 18.2; Origen, *Homilies on Jeremiah* 4.6; Origen, *Homilies on Ezekiel* 2.2; Origen, *Matthew* 12.43, 14.4; Origen, *Matthew* 54.119.

13. Origen, *First Principles* 2.7.3; Origen, *Matthew* 14.6; Origen, *Ezekiel* 2.2.

14. Origen, *Matthew* 16.12; Origen, *Matthew* 89; Origen, *Numbers* 3.2.

15. Origen, *First Principles* 4.3.4.

16. See 2 Corinthians 3:6. See Origen, *Song of Songs* 3.208.

17. Origen, *First Principles* 4.1.1; Origen, *Matthew* 27.

18. Origen, *First Principles* 4.2.4; Origen, *John* 6.227; Origen, *Leviticus* 1.1.

19. See Elizabeth A. Dively Lauro, *The Soul and Spirit of Scripture Within Origen's Exegesis* (Society of Biblical Literature, 2005), which is based on a doctoral thesis that challenges previous scholarly opinions and shows that there is a clear and consistent distinction between the two senses in Origen's writings.

20. Origen, *First Principles* 4.2.6. The references are to 1 Corinthians 9:9–10 and Deuteronomy 25:4.

21. Origen, *Homilies on Genesis* 8. See Genesis 22:1–14.

22. Origen, *Leviticus* 2.2.7.

23. Origen, *Genesis* 2. See Genesis 6:1–8:22.

24. See 1 Peter 3:20–21.

25. Origen, *Song of Songs* 1.4.

26. Origen, *Leviticus* 1.5.3.

27. Origen, *First Principles* 3.6.8, 4.3.13; Origen, *Commentary on Romans* 1.4.

28. Origen, *Song of Songs* 1.1.

29. Origen, *Homilies on Exodus* 5.5.

30. Origen, *First Principles* 4.3.1–3. See Genesis 1:14–19 and Matthew 5:29.

31. Origen, *First Principles* 4.2.9; Origen, *Against Celsus* 6.61–62.

32. Origen, *John* 20.329; Origen, *Matthew* 13.4.

33. Origen, *John* 28.56–58. See John 11:25–26.

34. Origen, *Matthew* 12.36–37. See Matthew 17:1–8.

35. Origen, *John* 1.45.

Chapter 3 Gregory of Nyssa

1. He did not come from Nyssa but became that town's bishop later in life and so is always associated with it, though it was of no particular importance either for him or for the church in general.

2. See 1 Corinthians 7:32–35.

3. This title has been given to only two other people—John, the author of the book of Revelation (known in the Western world as St. John the Divine), and a Byzantine writer called Symeon the New Theologian (949–1022), who is much less well-known in the West.

4. The word *homoousios* had existed before 325, but it had not been used in this theological sense.

5. See John 10:30.

6. See John 1:14; 15:26.

7. For an examination of this tendency, see Morwenna Ludlow, *Gregory of Nyssa, Ancient and (Post)modern* (Oxford University Press, 2007), who does her best to analyze and untangle the resulting confusion.

8. See 1 Samuel 28:12–14. Gregory wrote a treatise specifically on the subject.

9. See Matthew 2:1–12.

10. See Hebrews 11:8. Note that Gregory believed that Paul was the author of Hebrews.

11. Gregory of Nyssa, *Against Eunomius* 2.92. See Romans 1:17; 4:3.

12. See Plotinus, *Enneads* 6.9.8–11.

13. Plotinus, *Enneads* 5.8.22–23.

14. Gregory of Nyssa, *Life of Moses* 2.10–11. See Exodus 2:9–10.

15. Gregory of Nyssa, *Moses* 2.113–115. See Exodus 12:35–36.

16. Gregory of Nyssa, *Moses* 2.21. See Exodus 3:2.

17. Galatians 3:28. Note that Gregory took this verse out of context.

18. Gregory of Nyssa, *Dialogue with His Own Sister Macrina Concerning the Soul and the Resurrection* 46, col. 69.

19. Gregory of Nyssa, *Catechetical Orations* 26.

Chapter 4 Ambrosiaster

1. Augustine of Hippo, *Against the Pelagians* 4.4.7.

2. See Sophie Lunn-Rockliffe, *Ambrosiaster's Political Theology* (Oxford University Press, 2007), 19–26, for a discussion of this possibility.

3. Julian appears in his comment on 2 Thessalonians 2:7.

4. See his remarks on Ephesians 4:12.

5. Ambrosiaster, *Commentary on Romans* preface.

6. Ambrosiaster, *Romans* 1:9.

7. Ambrosiaster, *Romans* 1:17.

8. Ambrosiaster, *Romans* 2:3.

9. Ambrosiaster, *Romans* 2:8.

10. Ambrosiaster, *Romans* 2:9.

11. Ambrosiaster, *Romans* 4:12.

12. Ambrosiaster, *Romans* 5:13.

13. Ambrosiaster, *Romans* 5:13.

14. Ambrosiaster, *Romans* 5:14.

15. Ambrosiaster, *Commentary on 1 Corinthians* 11:7.

16. Ambrosiaster, *Romans* 16:13.

17. Ambrosiaster, *Romans* preface; Ambrosiaster, *Commentary on 2 Corinthians* 11:25. See Acts 27:42–44.

18. See Leviticus 19:18. It was also the teaching of Jesus, of course. See Matthew 22:39; Mark 12:31.

19. Ambrosiaster, *Romans* 13:9.
20. Ambrosiaster, *1 Corinthians* 8:11.
21. Ambrosiaster, *1 Corinthians* 14:4–5.
22. Ambrosiaster, *1 Corinthians* 12:11.

Chapter 5 John Chrysostom

1. John must have been born sometime between 344 and 354. The date 349 is the midpoint between these two and its probability has been defended by J. N. D. Kelly, *Golden Mouth: The Story of John Chrysostom—Ascetic, Preacher, Bishop* (Baker, 1995), 296–98.
2. The Greek word *synkatabasis* is literally "condescension," a word that is sometimes used to describe this, though it tends to have a somewhat pejorative meaning in modern English. Another possibility is "adaptation." For a detailed study of the subject, see David Rylaarsdam, *John Chrysostom on Divine Pedagogy: The Coherence of His Theology and Preaching* (Oxford University Press, 2014).
3. For John, as for the apostle Paul, the terms "Jew" and "Greek" were religious more than ethnic descriptors, despite the obvious overlap between them.
4. See Acts 16:3.
5. John Chrysostom, *In principium Actorum* 4.
6. See Matthew 26:39, where Jesus prayed that the Father's will, and not his, should be done.
7. John Chrysostom, *Homilies on John* 34.2.
8. John Chrysostom, *John* 41.1.
9. John Chrysostom, *John* 55.2. See John 8:56.
10. Six homilies on Isaiah 6 have survived in Greek, along with extensive fragments from Isaiah 1–8 and 10.
11. This number does not include Galatians, because what survives is a combined commentary on the entire book. It must originally have been a sermon series, which would bring the total number to well over 250.
12. It should also be remembered that Paul's hometown of Tarsus is not far from Antioch and that Antioch was the base for Paul's early missionary journeys. The two men were almost compatriots, even though they lived more than three centuries apart.
13. Any similarities with modern academia are of course entirely coincidental!
14. See 1 Corinthians 1:26–31.
15. John Chrysostom, *John* 2.2.
16. It must be remembered that John lived at a time before baptism had become universal and automatic. The people he baptized knew what they believed and understood that to become a Christian was to separate oneself from wider (pagan) society. It was only later, when the church and the wider society virtually fused into one, that baptism was reduced to a formality dissociated from genuine spiritual power.

Notes

Chapter 6 Theodore of Mopsuestia

1. See Richard Price, ed., *The Acts of the Council of Constantinople of 553* (Liverpool University Press, 2009) for a complete history of this council.

2. The Creed of Nicaea was the one adopted in 325 and must be distinguished from the Nicene Creed that we use today that was written in 381 or later.

3. See D. S. Wallace-Hadrill, *Christian Antioch: A Study of Early Christian Thought in the East* (Cambridge University Press, 1982), 45–51, for the details.

4. Theodore of Mopsuestia, *Commentary on Malachi*.

5. Theodore of Mopsuestia, *Malachi*.

6. Recorded by the fourth session of the Second Council of Constantinople, 77–78 (LXVIII–LXIX), in Price, *Council of Constantinople*, 265.

7. Theodore of Mopsuestia, *Commentary on Psalms 1–81*.

8. For Diodore's interpretation, see Robert C. Hill, ed., *Diodore of Tarsus: Commentary on Psalms 1–51* (Society of Biblical Literature Press, 2005), 165–70.

9. For a discussion of this, see Robert C. Hill, *Reading the Old Testament in Antioch* (Society of Biblical Literature Press, 2005), 179.

10. Theodore of Mopsuestia, *Commentary on the Twelve Minor Prophets*. See 1 Corinthians 15:55.

11. Theodore of Mopsuestia, *Twelve Minor Prophets*. See Matthew 21:5; John 12:15.

12. Theodore of Mopsuestia, *Twelve Minor Prophets*.

13. Theodore of Mopsuestia, *Twelve Minor Prophets*. See Luke 11:29–30.

14. See Hosea 1:2–3.

15. See Isaiah 20:2–6. Isaiah couldn't have been totally "naked" in the modern sense, since in that case there would have been no need to mention that he was bare-foot. It probably means that he was stripped to his underwear, as we might say today.

16. Theodore of Mopsuestia, *Twelve Minor Prophets*.

17. Theodore of Mopsuestia, *Twelve Minor Prophets*.

18. Theodore of Mopsuestia, *Twelve Minor Prophets*. See Acts 2:17, and also Theodore's comments on Haggai 2:5, where a similar issue arises.

19. Theodore of Mopsuestia, *Commentary on the Gospel of John*, trans. M. Conti (InterVarsity Press, 2010), 56.

20. Theodore of Mopsuestia, *Commentary on John*, 95.

21. Theodore of Mopsuestia, *Commentary on the Pauline Epistles*.

Chapter 7 Jerome

1. Some scholars, including J. N. D. Kelly in his biography, give his date of birth as 331, but it is now generally agreed that this is too early.

2. *Vulgate* means "popular" and should not be confused with the related word "vulgar."

3. There had, however, been a revision in the late sixteenth century, though it was considered to be a return to Jerome's original text and not something entirely new.

Notes

Chapter 6 Theodore of Mopsuestia

1. See Richard Price, ed., *The Acts of the Council of Constantinople of 553* (Liverpool University Press, 2009) for a complete history of this council.

2. The Creed of Nicaea was the one adopted in 325 and must be distinguished from the Nicene Creed that we use today that was written in 381 or later.

3. See D. S. Wallace-Hadrill, *Christian Antioch: A Study of Early Christian Thought in the East* (Cambridge University Press, 1982), 45–51, for the details.

4. Theodore of Mopsuestia, *Commentary on Malachi*.

5. Theodore of Mopsuestia, *Malachi*.

6. Recorded by the fourth session of the Second Council of Constantinople, 77–78 (LXVIII–LXIX), in Price, *Council of Constantinople*, 265.

7. Theodore of Mopsuestia, *Commentary on Psalms 1–81*.

8. For Diodore's interpretation, see Robert C. Hill, ed., *Diodore of Tarsus: Commentary on Psalms 1–51* (Society of Biblical Literature Press, 2005), 165–70.

9. For a discussion of this, see Robert C. Hill, *Reading the Old Testament in Antioch* (Society of Biblical Literature Press, 2005), 179.

10. Theodore of Mopsuestia, *Commentary on the Twelve Minor Prophets*. See 1 Corinthians 15:55.

11. Theodore of Mopsuestia, *Twelve Minor Prophets*. See Matthew 21:5; John 12:15.

12. Theodore of Mopsuestia, *Twelve Minor Prophets*.

13. Theodore of Mopsuestia, *Twelve Minor Prophets*. See Luke 11:29–30.

14. See Hosea 1:2–3.

15. See Isaiah 20:2–6. Isaiah couldn't have been totally "naked" in the modern sense, since in that case there would have been no need to mention that he was bare-foot. It probably means that he was stripped to his underwear, as we might say today.

16. Theodore of Mopsuestia, *Twelve Minor Prophets*.

17. Theodore of Mopsuestia, *Twelve Minor Prophets*.

18. Theodore of Mopsuestia, *Twelve Minor Prophets*. See Acts 2:17, and also Theodore's comments on Haggai 2:5, where a similar issue arises.

19. Theodore of Mopsuestia, *Commentary on the Gospel of John*, trans. M. Conti (InterVarsity Press, 2010), 56.

20. Theodore of Mopsuestia, *Commentary on John*, 95.

21. Theodore of Mopsuestia, *Commentary on the Pauline Epistles*.

Chapter 7 Jerome

1. Some scholars, including J. N. D. Kelly in his biography, give his date of birth as 331, but it is now generally agreed that this is too early.

2. *Vulgate* means "popular" and should not be confused with the related word "vulgar."

3. There had, however, been a revision in the late sixteenth century, though it was considered to be a return to Jerome's original text and not something entirely new.

212

4. For a discussion of these commentaries and the possible reasons why Jerome wrote them, see Andrew Cain, *Jerome's Commentaries on the Pauline Epistles and the Architecture of Exegetical Authority* (Oxford University Press, 2018).

5. Jerome knew that his order was not that of the Hebrew Bible or the Septuagint, and he said so in the preface to his commentary on Nahum, though without explaining his own choice. See Jerome, *Commentaries on the Twelve Prophets* (InterVarsity Press, 2016), 1:1.

6. Jerome, *Epistles* 106.55.

7. By way of comparison, the English Standard Version (ESV) has "house" in all of these verses, though sometimes in a slightly more precise form. For example, in Isaiah 39:2 it uses both "treasure house" and "storehouses" for *cella* and *apotheca* respectively.

8. See Matthew 5:18.

9. Even modern translators find this hard to deal with. The ESV, for example, puts "emasculate" instead of "castrate," perhaps hoping that the less familiar word will blunt the force of what Paul actually said.

10. Thomas Scheck, trans., *St. Jerome's Commentaries on Galatians, Titus, and Philemon* (University of Notre Dame Press, 2010), 217–18.

11. Augustine of Hippo, *Commentary on Galatians*, trans. Eric Plumer (Oxford University Press, 2003), 203.

12. See Matthew 19:12.

13. Scheck, *Commentaries*, 97–98.

14. See Acts 10:1–29.

15. See Acts 16:3; 18:18; and 21:23–26, all of which Jerome referred to. He also quoted Paul as saying that he became a Jew to the Jews in order to win them for Christ (1 Cor. 9:20).

16. Augustine of Hippo, *Epistles* 40.

17. Augustine of Hippo, *Galatians*, 145.

18. The most famous example of this was the angel's directive to Mary and Joseph to name their son Jesus, because he would save his people from their sins (Matt. 1:21). But the principle is found throughout the Old Testament.

19. Jerome, *Twelve Minor Prophets*, 1:75.

20. Jerome, *Twelve Minor Prophets*, 2:151.

21. Jerome, *Twelve Minor Prophets*, 2:117. The fall of souls from heaven refers to their preexistence in eternity.

22. Jerome, *Twelve Minor Prophets*, 2:124. He was commenting on Malachi 1:10–13.

23. Jerome, *Twelve Minor Prophets*, 2:125.

24. Jerome, *Twelve Minor Prophets*, 2:201.

25. The ESV says, "The stone will cry out from the wall, and the beam from the woodwork respond."

26. Jerome, *Twelve Minor Prophets*, 1:204–5.

27. Jerome, *Twelve Minor Prophets*, 2:206.

28. Jerome, *Twelve Minor Prophets*, 2:207.

Chapter 8 Augustine of Hippo

1. A loose translation of Tertullian, *Apology* 50.13.

2. By "British" we mean what would nowadays be called "Welsh," that is to say, Celtic rather than Anglo-Saxon. The Romans did not abandon their British provinces until 410, after which the Anglo-Saxons arrived and created the England that we know today.

3. By "city" Augustine meant what we would call "society" or "community." Babylon and Rome were both cities (in the modern sense), but they were empires too. Even today, we sometimes speak of Moscow or Beijing when we mean Russia or China—the capital city represents the country as a whole.

4. See Romans 11:16–24.

5. See Genesis 1:26–27.

6. Augustine of Hippo, *Tractate on John's Gospel* 80.3.

7. Church of England, "Articles of Religion," https://www.churchofengland.org/prayer-and-worship/worship-texts-and-resources/book-common-prayer/articles-religion.

8. Those familiar with the Westminster Shorter Catechism, widely used among Presbyterians, will remember the first question, "What is the chief end of man?," and the answer, "Man's chief end is to glorify God *and to enjoy him for ever*" (italics mine). This comes straight out of Augustine.

9. See also 1 Peter 2:2 and Hebrews 5:12–14.

10. He got this from what Paul said in 1 Corinthians 13:13, of course.

11. Augustine of Hippo, *Exposition of the Psalms* 137.12. See 1 Corinthians 10:4.

12. The works of Augustine are for the most part readily available in a range of translations. New City Press in New York is publishing *The Works of Saint Augustine: A Translation for the 21st Century*, which is now very near completion. One problem with it is that the translators have often chosen English titles that are not immediately obvious—for example, *De doctrina Christiana* is *Teaching Christianity*.

Chapter 9 Cyril of Alexandria

1. Socrates, *Ecclesiastical History* 7.15.

2. See, for example, Cyril of Alexandria, *Paschal Homily* 17.

3. See J. A. McGuckin, *St. Cyril of Alexandria and the Christological Controversy* (St. Vladimir's Seminary Press, 2004), 273–75, for the complete text.

4. Sabellianism was named after an obscure man called Sabellius, who supposedly taught that the divine *hypostases* had no real existence but represented only three different functions of the one God (e.g., creator, redeemer, sanctifier). For that reason, it is also known as "modalism," the functions being regarded as "modes" of the divine being.

5. Modern chapter divisions were devised in Paris around 1200, and verses first appeared just after the Reformation in the sixteenth century.

6. Cyril of Alexandria, *Commentary on John's Gospel* 3.

Notes

7. Cyril of Alexandria, *John's Gospel* 3.
8. Cyril of Alexandria, *John's Gospel* 3.
9. Cyril of Alexandria, *John's Gospel* 3.

Chapter 10 Theodoret of Cyrrhus

1. Some scholars believe that Leo has been given too much credit for this, but that need not concern us here.
2. Chalcedon is a suburb of Constantinople, on the Asian side of the Bosphorus. Today it is called Kadıköy in Turkish.
3. This is not just an arcane theological argument. It is possible for a human being to lose their will (in a coma, for example), without ceasing to be a person. This has considerable implications for things like euthanasia, where the will of the individual concerned may not be ascertainable, but their personhood remains inviolate.
4. See Gerald L. Bray, *A History of Christian Theology: A Trinitarian Approach* (Crossway, 2024), 361–62.
5. For example, his commentary on Isaiah, discovered in 1899, was not edited until 1932. A three-volume French translation appeared in 1981 to 1984, and an English one as recently as 2026.
6. Quotation adapted from Robert C. Hill, *Reading the Old Testament in Antioch* (Society of Biblical Literature Press, 2005), 158.
7. See Hill, *Reading the Old Testament*, 176.
8. See 1 Corinthians 10:4. In commenting on that passage, Theodoret was determined to point out that it was not the rock itself that was Christ, but that it was used by God as a means of showing his grace to the people. The link between the rock and Jesus was therefore one of grace, not of substance.
9. See Hill, *Reading the Old Testament*, 176–77.

Gerald Bray (DLitt, University of Paris-Sorbonne) is research professor of divinity at Beeson Divinity School in Birmingham, Alabama, and director of research at Latimer Trust, Oak Hill College, London. A prolific author, he has written many books, including *God Is Love*, *The Doctrine of God*, *A History of Christian Theology*, *Athens and Jerusalem*, *The History of Christianity in Britain and Ireland*, and *Biblical Interpretation: Past and Present*. Bray is a minister in the Church of England and was editor of the Anglican journal *Churchman* from 1983 to 2018.